LIFE'S TOO SHORT

LIFE'S TOO SHORT

A Memoir

DARIUS RUCKER

WITH ALAN EISENSTOCK

DEYST.

An Imprint of WILLIAM MORROW

DEYST.

FIRST EDITION

Designed by Jennifer Chung

Library of Congress Cataloging-in-Publication Data has been applied for.

ISBN 978-0-06-323874-9

24 25 26 27 28 LBC 5 4 3 2 1

In memory of my mother, Carolyn,
    who always encouraged me to sing,
and for my family,
    who means everything to me.
Life's too short, get to livin'.
        —Darius Rucker

I've been lost, I've been found

I left my mark on my little bitty town . . .

If I ever get to Heaven, I'm gonna have a story to tell . . .

Got some parts gonna make you laugh, some parts gonna make you cry . . .

Some pages I wish I could tear out, but I ain't gonna lie . . .

Because it's the story of my life.

"Story to Tell"
Darius Rucker
Ross Copperman
Ashley Gorley

CONTENTS

INTRODUCTION ("PIECES OF MY LIFE")

Elvis Presley

Music.

Music.

Seems obvious, I suppose, but when I think about my life—telling my story—that's what it's all about. From the beginning until now.

The music.

Not the fame, or the fun, or the crowds, or the career. Or the sex, drink, drugs, and money.

No.

The music.

In fact, if I look back at my life, and I try to see into my past, everything seems blurry. At least at first. I have to squint and blink away the haze so I can visualize the events that shaped me and the people who meant so much to me. I start to see clearly the people who swept through my life, for better or for worse, most of them giving so much to me, a couple of them taking a part of me. At first I don't really see them. I can't make out their faces. Then I lean into my past and I hear something, a sound begins, reverberating in my mind, faintly at first, then louder, and I realize what it is.

Music.

I start to hear it. It comes on. Pours into me.

Songs.

I hear the songs.

Melodies. Chords. Harmonies. Lyrics. Then as all those elements fill in I start to hear something more. I begin to hear the stories that make up the songs, the stories that the songs tell.

Gradually everything starts to clear up. A fog lifts. I look back and through the music I can see.

And when I say I look back, I'm talking *way* back, fifty-plus years, when I was a kid. A little kid. Four years old. I started to hear the music then, that long ago. I heard the music loud and clear. I hear it now. I hear it always.

The music would float around me, then flow into me, zap through my body like an electric charge, and lift me. I would soar. I would fly. I'm four years old, sitting at our kitchen table, my head bent over, leaning into the radio, listening, even as I'm surrounded by other sounds, other voices, my mother, my grandmother, my sisters, my brother, but I wouldn't hear them. I wouldn't even be there. I would be somewhere else. Lost in the music. Devoured by the sound. Transported by the songs.

It's always—*always*—about the music.

Specifically, certain songs, each one having a profound effect on me. To paraphrase the sage and soulful Ronnie Spector, each one of those songs is a little piece of my life.

That's why I need to tell you my story through the songs that meant the most to me—the songs that coursed through my life, the songs that formed me, that took me higher, deeper, farther than any words, visual image, vision, or dream could take me. When a song hit me, my life stopped. I would hear a song—at age five, or ten, or fifteen, or twenty—and I would listen to it. And that's all I would do, for hours. Sometimes for days. I wouldn't just listen to the song. I would *live* in that song. I would hear a song and I would listen to it again, and again, and again. I would lose track of time, of space. I would become submerged in that song. The song would become my world.

This book is about my life as told through those songs. Songs that took me away, starting at ground level, living in a poor but happy home, never wanting much more, enjoying what I had, even when times got tough, because I had my escape, my refuge. I had my music. My songs. Songs that nobody else in my life could hear, at least not in the way I could. The songs would take me to places I could never dream. I would feel myself rising to heights I could never imagine, daring myself to stay at the height, and then go higher, and higher, and higher, until I arrived at a place I never knew existed. I found myself flying, floating, and then, after a while, I would start teetering, and begin to fall, then I'd plummet, end over end, hurtling back down, somehow—barely— preventing a headfirst crash into earth. More than once. And then, again, I'd envelop myself in music. A song would rise, and again the song would save me.

What songs? What kind of music? Everything. An eclectic and surprising soundtrack. All different—different songs, different melodies, different genres, different styles. I lived inside my own personal playlist. Pop. Country. Rap. Soul. Rock.

The Beatles. Stevie Wonder. Al Green. Frank Sinatra. R.E.M. Nanci Griffith. The Notorious B.I.G. Lou Reed. KISS. Barry Manilow. And more.

I listened to them all.

They all formed me.

Molding me into the singer I became.

Into the person I am.

The music was my pulse, my motor, my passion, my obsession, my religion. The songs were holy. The songs made me *me*.

I've picked out twenty-three songs for you, twenty-three essential songs. They're not in the exact order that I heard them, or remember them, but pretty close. They all took me to a place I'd never been before. They transported me. They all meant the world to me.

Even more, they all meant my life.

So, please, hear the music.

Stand next to me. Clap your hands. Snap your fingers. Close your eyes. Hear my songs. Hear them with me.

Lose yourself in them.

Let them take you away.

Let them take you home.

1

"DROWNING"
Hootie & The Blowfish

t's 1998 or 1999. Not sure. I know it's at least four years since David Letterman made us a household name, and after *cracked rear view* shocked the music world, selling more than a million copies a month, and we'd ridden that rocket ship, arriving on the planet ubiquitous, toured the world, more than once, and then, boom, kind of soft-landed back to earth. Still, everyone knows our name. Yeah, it's early 1999. Pretty sure. Maybe. As I say, time back then has gone fuzzy. Well, a lot of stuff back then has gone fuzzy. When we were on the road, I spent most of my hours holed up with the guys, listening to music and smoking, snorting, or swallowing various reality-altering indulgences—mushrooms, Mollies, acid, to name a few—nearly always accompanied by my close personal friend Jim Beam. If I'm honest—and I will be completely honest—Hootie & The Blowfish reigned supreme in two not altogether unrelated areas: selling records and doing drugs. One time, a roadie, British guy who had worked with several rock and roll bands known for their contribution to the music world as well as their record-breaking drug consumption, stared at the mountain range of the snowy-peaked white powder we'd laid out on the table in front of us, and said, "I've been around a lot of bands and nobody comes close to you guys, not *close*." Not sure if he was complimentary or amazed. I was too high to decide. Anyway, those days we played stadiums at night, night after night, and smoked and snorted and drank the rest of the time. We partied hard, all of us, except Mark. For the rest of us, the party never stopped. Until it did.

Along the way, I got tight with Woody. Woody Harrelson. Fantastic actor. An even better human being. Pot smoker supreme, major mushroom enjoyer, beautiful guy. Not sure how we became friends. I think he came to a show. He popped in backstage afterward and we hit it off. That's as much as we remember. Truth is, everybody wants to be friends with Woody. He's kind, generous, fun, and mellow. When I tell him that he's the mellowest guy I know, Woody takes the drumstick-sized joint I'm offering him and says, "I'm not mellow. I'm just lazy as shit."

Around this time, the band has released our third album, *Musical Chairs*. We've been touring nonstop, on the road constantly, finally coming to the last leg of back-to-back tour stops, and I'm fried. I need a break. Woody, who lives in Hawaii, sees how stressed I am and invites me to hang out with him and chill. I've never been to Woody's house, but he's shown me pictures. Massive palms and coconut trees lining his land. Flowers and vegetation everywhere. A house with breathtaking views in every direction. He starts to describe some of the activities we'll enjoy, but I say yes before he can finish his sentence.

I head to Hawaii, preparing to stay with Woody for two weeks.

I'm not prepared for Woody's lifestyle.

Woody lives in the middle of nowhere, far from any people. The house sits on a stunning piece of property, a flat, grassy pocket overlooking a series of cliffs, and I might be jet-lagged or stoned, but inside his home, I don't see *walls*. Lots of open area. Views from every window, above and below. And those cliffs. Stunningly imposing, beautiful, and straight down, the waves crashing, thundering below.

The house itself isn't huge, maybe two thousand square feet. That's because the main guest quarters are *outside*. All over his wide yard, he's set up several yurts. A yurt, I learn, is a tricked-out circular tent, the walls fashioned from cloth or canvas or maybe wool. I don't know. I don't care. I start to head into the house, but Woody steers me to his lawn, back to the yurts.

"This is where all my guests stay, except you," he says, stopping at one of the largest yurts, grinning that famous infectious Woody smile. "Very comfortable."

"They don't stay in the house?"

"This is better."

"A fucking tent?"

"No, man. A *yurt*. It's how the Mongolian people used to live. You hungry?"

"I'm starving."

"Chill out here. I'll be right back with a snack."

I check out the yurt. I look around at the accommodations. Blankets cover a low bed, a kind of futon. The yurt has running water, a bathroom, electricity, and furniture that's functional and comfortable. I've never been a fan of camping, but this yurt goes way beyond camping. It's almost luxurious. Almost.

A minute later, Woody arrives with a ceramic bowl filled with purple paste. He sits cross-legged on the blankets on the floor of the yurt. I join him.

"Try this," he says.

He dips his hand into the bowl, scoops out three fingers of purple goo, and licks the gunk off.

"Hits the spot," he says, offering me the bowl. "Go for it."

"I'm really not that hungry," I say.

"It's poi. Try it."

I do. Reluctantly. The goo tastes like blueberry Spackle.

"Well?"

"Yum," I say.

"It'll grow on you."

"I don't think so."

"So, a heads-up. We start every day with yoga. Clothing optional. Actually, clothing discouraged."

I take this in, nod. "Naked yoga."

"Yeah. First, a group chant, then naked yoga, then a poi drink."

I nod at the purple paste in the bowl. "What do you do? Run this through a blender, pour it into a glass, and then drink it?"

"Exactly. Got to flush out those toxins. Oh, and get used to it. No TV."

I hear a sound escape from my mouth, something between a whimper and a wail.

"Man, you are stressed."

"A tad. Yeah."

"I know what you need. Let's fire up a hooter."

We head into the house, to my room, and we smoke a blunt the size of an eggplant. In a few minutes, I'm mellow as hell. A few minutes after that, I'm conked out. I sleep for twelve hours.

The next day, I give in to Woody's world.

I get up at dawn and do coed naked yoga with Woody and a group of strangers. I drink my pasty purple poi drink. Woody and I take walks. We talk. We laugh. We play chess. I'm decent, Woody's a master. And, yes, we smoke dope.

For lunch every day, we eat salads made from roots, flowers, fruit, and plants that his cook picks right from his garden and off his trees. For a snack, we have poi. I don't love it, but I get used to it. For dinner, more salad. We never cook anything. We eat everything fresh and raw. A few days pass. I feel like I'm in some foreign land, adjusting to the native customs. But you know what? I love it. I feel so relaxed. And I feel different. I feel—changed.

. . .

One afternoon, on a typically cloudless, crystal-blue-sky, slightly breezy, seventy-degree day in paradise, Woody suggests that we go swimming. A friend of his, Kirk, has recently taken up residence in one of the yurts and Woody has invited him along.

"All this chilling is great," Woody says, "but you gotta get your blood up."

At Woody's, if you want to go swimming, you don't simply slip on your trunks and dive into the pool. Way more complicated than that. We begin our swim by climbing down a jagged cliff—*very* slowly and carefully, inch by inch—until after a treacherous twenty-five-minute descent, we arrive at a sliver of a beach tucked into the lip of a sleepy-looking lagoon. We catch our breath as the water laps gently at our feet. Shading my eyes with my hand, I peer at a small strip of land in the distance.

"What's that, Woody?"

"That's where we're going. It's a little island."

"Cool," I say. I step into the water. "Wow. This is like bathwater."

"It is."

"And so calm."

"It isn't."

I look at him.

"Are you a good swimmer?" Woody asks.

"Pretty decent, yeah."

"Here's the deal. We're going straight out to that island. Dive in and swim out. That's all you got to do. Go straight. That's the main thing. Make sure you go straight. Because if you swim toward the beach or the rocks, you'll get caught in the current and it will take you *into* the rocks, and you'll be fucked."

I cock my head toward Woody. This is by far the longest and most pointed speech he's ever given me. I keep staring at him.

"Darius. You hear me?"

"Yeah."

"Stay out of the current. Swim straight out, okay?"

"Okay, yeah, I got you, man."

Whap. Splash.

Woody and Kirk dive in side by side, slicing the water together like a pair of synchronized swimmers. I hesitate half a second, and then I dive in right behind them.

At least I think I do.

I begin swimming, and, in all modesty, I'm better than a decent swimmer. I'm a strong, confident swimmer. I was born and raised in South Carolina, home to some of the best beaches in the country—Hilton Head, Kiawah Island, Sullivan's Island, Folly Beach. I know them all. I swam at them all. I know my way around a beach.

I cut through the water, swimming powerfully, heading straight out, as Woody said. But as I swim—straight ahead, I swear I'm going straight ahead—I start to feel disoriented. I don't see Woody or Kirk. I don't see the small island that's supposed to be right in front of me. I don't see—anything. I keep swimming straight, but all I see is water. Everywhere. As far as I can see, my horizon is filled with water. Then I look to my right and squint and I finally see something familiar. The rock cliff. Yes. I recognize the jagged rocks. That's where we started, right there at that cliff. I know one thing from my years of swimming at beaches. At the bottom of every rock cliff lies a beach. Always. Even a tiny sliver of a beach. Count on it.

I turn in the direction of the cliff.

I hoist myself and dive into the water and I swim.

I open my eyes below the surface and all I see are fish. A shit ton of fish. Swirling everywhere. Enveloping me. Dancing, skittering around me. I rise out of the water and look toward the cliff.

I see no cliff.

I see no beach.

I see nothing but water.

I panic.

Dude, I say to myself, *just swim. Like Woody said. Just fucking swim.*

I calm myself and start to swim, my strokes strong, determined, confident, and I glide—*oh, yeah, I got this. No problem.* I lift myself up, and—

The current pulls me back down.

Rips me backward.

I try another stroke, using every ounce of force I can find.

But I'm caught.

The current grips me around my torso and yanks me down.

I'll fight it. I'll fight my way out of here.

The current pulls me harder.

The current is ferocious. I feel as if some horrific giant squid has lashed itself around my body, circling and tightening its tentacles around my legs, dragging me under the water.

I gulp and I gasp and I keep fighting.

I fight and flail for I have no idea how long—ten minutes, fifteen—and then I hear a voice.

Woody.

I can't see him, but I hear him. He's not far.

"Darius!"

I nod, unable to speak, and some water splashes near me, then a spray like rain douses my forehead, and I see Woody. He swims up next to me. "You okay?"

"I'm fine, but I can't get out of this current."

"Alright, don't worry, we'll get out of here."

"Good."

"No worries. We got this." Woody rises up and waves his hand. "Yo, Kirk! Over here! *Kirk!*"

"Does he see us?"

"Yeah, no, I don't think so. Let's just swim."

We thrust ourselves forward, trying to swim straight, but we can't move. We're swimming in circles, thrashing, going nowhere. Then Woody, breathing hard, nods, and begins treading water. I nod with him, keeping time with the bobbing of his head, and I follow his lead, the two of us caught in this vortex, slapping our arms, staying in place, not advancing, just treading water, for ten, fifteen, twenty, thirty minutes.

"Kirk doesn't see us," I say feebly, my arms aching, pain piercing my forearms.

"Not yet," Woody admits. "Keep treading water. Just stay afloat."

I keep flapping my arms, staying in place, keeping the current at bay, but I feel like I have a fifty-pound weight strapped to each arm. I can't lift my arms anymore. I feel so tired. Beyond tired. I feel myself drifting away.

And then everything turns a shocking shade of pure white—a blinding blast of white—and I see—a vision. Right in front of me. I see—

My mom.

Can't be.

My mom died in 1992—seven years ago—but I see her clearly. I see her kind and loving face, her sparkling, happy eyes. She is walking toward me, stepping gently, almost airily, on tiptoe, and she tilts her head, reaches her arms out to me, and she smiles.

"Mom, I see you," I say. "I'm coming to you."

Then—*whap*—in rapid motion, moments from my life flicker before me like quick cuts in a movie. In each one, I feel my purpose, my essence, I'm doing what I do that defines me, that fills me as much as my breath—

I'm singing.

In a club, belting "So. Central Rain," my favorite R.E.M. song, a drunken frat pack and a crush of sorority sisters crammed in tight in front of us, an overflowing crowd overwhelming the tiny stage, the entire off-key, drunken college chorus howling along to the song's chorus—*"I'm sorrrrry"*—the room pulsing with heat and the whir of Mark's guitar and the throb of Dean's bass and the crash of Soni's drums, a pungent mix of sweat, perfume, and pot filling up the room, the smells slamming me back, making me wired, making me high.

I'm singing.

In a recording studio, laying down the track to "Hold My Hand," my mouth hovering over the microphone, oversized headphones cupping my ears, my eyes closed tight, trying to get the song exactly right, knowing in my heart that I have, and then opening my eyes and seeing David Crosby, from Crosby, Stills, Nash & Young, standing a few feet away, singing harmony to our song, on our first album.

I'm singing.

At night, belting out "Let Her Cry" in a stadium filled with a massive, cheering crowd, fifty thousand people, all on their feet, every single person singing along with me, each one holding a lighter aloft, the tiny flames dotting the darkness, surrounding us, embracing us, making the night look like it's filled with an infinite number of fireflies.

And—I'm singing.

In my mom's hospital room, holding her hand, my voice raw and cracking with sadness and fear as I power my way through Nanci Griffith's "I Wish It Would Rain," my mom unconscious, her head softly indenting her pillow, her face motionless, her eyes closed, her breathing steady and low, but I can feel something between us—an electrical connection. I know she can hear me, I *know* it, so I sing, and I sing, and I keep singing, refusing to leave her bedside, refusing to let go of her hand, believing she can hear my voice and somehow my singing will cure her, or awaken her, or that at least my voice, if nothing else, will calm her, soothe her, ease her pain.

All these moments flash by in a blink and then—

I'm back in the lagoon, the water swallowing me, my body caught in the vortex, the current tugging at my legs. I'm barely able to lift my arms. My forearms flap limply as I try to tread water, trying, trying—failing—and I look over at Woody, and I take in his face, and I know instantly, without a doubt, that I am going to die.

"Woody," I say. "You got to let me go, man. You got to let me go."

"What are you talking about?"

"Dude—"

I can't finish. It's so hard to speak. I swallow and try to catch my breath, but I start panting.

"There's no reason," I whisper.

The words leak out of my mouth, one at a time, each syllable a tiny jab of air, causing me to gasp. I blow out a final burst of words.

"This is it."

"This is what?" Woody says.

"The way it ends. How I'm gonna die. Woody, go back. There's no reason for both of us to die right here."

"Darius. Dude. Stop that, man."

"I'm not making it out of here, man. I'm exhausted. I couldn't climb out of here right now if I wanted to. I got nothing left."

Then I feel Woody coming closer to me. Knifing through the water to my side. He tucks his face next to mine, chin to chin, closer than an inch away. I feel the flutter of his breath on my cheek. Then he speaks and I hear Woody from *Cheers,* simple, direct, a little goofy.

"*Die?* Shit. Not on my watch."

I start to speak, but then I see something in the distance—a vision? A mirage? An angel? I see—a human form, a swimmer, coming toward us. Coming closer . . . closer . . . closer . . .

Woody rises out of the water, shooting straight up, frantically thrusting both arms in the air like a referee signaling a touchdown, before he crashes back into the water with a violent splash.

"Kirk," Woody says to me. "He's coming."

From that moment until I land on the tiny beach, alive, my mind has gone blank. I have no memory of the next few minutes. All I know for sure is that somehow Woody pulls me out of the current and he and Kirk drag me back to the beach because here I am, twenty-five years later.

But one tiny speck of memory does stick in my mind as I lie on that thin slice of beach.

"Woody," I say. "I just want to go back to dry land."

"You've been through a lot," Woody says. "Know what? I think I'll let you watch TV tonight."

"Fire up the bong," I say, the last thing I remember.

. . .

During the second week, I get antsy. I love Woody's world, but I'm starting to miss my world, or as I call it, civilization.

"Woody," I tell him. "I have to return to the real world. Just for a day or two. I have to play golf. I really do."

"I hear you. I think Willie's home. I'll call him."

I pace in the living room as Woody calls his buddy Willie Nelson. After a few rings, Willie answers.

Woody says, "Hey, man, how you doing—"

I snatch the phone from Woody. "Willie, it's Darius. Listen. I'm at Woody's and I need to play some golf. Can I please come over and play golf with you? Please?"

"Definitely. Kris is here, too. Come on over, stay a few days, we'll play golf, we'll play cards, I'll fix you right up."

"Thank you, man. Thank you."

Woody and I drive to Willie's house, a couple hours away. We wind our way up a treacherous mountain road lined with tropical plants and flowers and arrive around dinnertime. We park outside the front entrance of his sprawling compound, which is nestled into groves of mango, avocado, and papaya trees and tucked into the slope of a long-dormant volcano. I glimpse my favorite feature—a lush and inviting nine-hole golf course. Willie's front door, as you would expect, is open. As we enter the front hall, Willie greets us from the top of a staircase. He grins down at us, fanning away a cloud of smoke that he's just exhaled from a joint the size of a baby's thigh.

"Darius," Willie says, his smile wide and warm. "How long you been at Woody's?"

"Twelve days."

"Going on two weeks," Willie says. "You need some meat, don't you?"

"Oh, man," I say.

"Burgers and hot dogs. How's that sound?"

"I think I might cry."

I stay at Willie's for two days. I eat meat. I play poker. I get high. And both days, Willie, Kris Kristofferson, and I play golf. Did I mention that I eat meat?

I'm in heaven.

Figuratively.

Because thanks to Woody Harrelson, I'm here, back on earth, alive.

2

"FOR THE GOOD TIMES"

Al Green

Nineteen seventy-two.

Charleston, South Carolina.

A chilly evening in mid-November.

I lie spread out on the floor of our living room, listening to Al Green on the stereo.

I am six years old.

Curled up into the music, I practically hug the massive maple-wood hi-fi console, the centerpiece of the room—the most important item of furniture in the house, more important than my *bed,* as far as I'm concerned. The console has two doors in front, opening to an AM/FM radio on one side and a turntable on the other. A built-in speaker fills the rest of the inside, with controls to adjust volume, treble, and bass. I blast the volume, going heavy on the bass, approaching max. The way it should be. I like the volume up high so that the music enters my eardrums and rumbles through my entire body, head to toe, like a pulse. My mom has set up the living room with a cushy couch and a couple of overstuffed armchairs, but I never sit on any of them. I camp out right here on the floor, as close to the hi-fi and music as I can get. I'd stick my head into the console if I could. I want to get *inside* the music.

It's Friday night and I'm the only one in here. Carolyn, my mother, has invited three friends to join her for an evening of a light supper, Budweiser, maybe some cards, and definitely gossip. Her friends, for the moment gathered in the kitchen, which is adjacent to the living room, have all come straight from work. My mother, an OB-GYN nurse, hasn't had time to change out of her pale blue uniform. The ladies have poured their first round of Buds and have begun to sip their beers and nibble on some snacks. My mother—short, genuine, hilarious, a force of nature, the ringleader—says something and all four of the ladies burst into laughter. Their voices roar, ebb, the ladies sip their drinks again, and then my mom leads her friends into the living room.

My three sisters and my brother have made themselves scarce, which they always do when my mother entertains. Funny. I never do. I love when my mom invites her friends over. I like hanging out with adults. I enjoy watching these ladies giving in to the weekend, allowing themselves to loosen up, laugh, enjoy an adult beverage or two. But I mainly love seeing my mom so happy. She works long hours, often taking double shifts, even triple shifts, to make ends meet. Even at six years old, I'm aware of how tight money can be, how close we occasionally come to teetering at the financial edge. For a single mom, raising, feeding, clothing her own five kids and sometimes putting up other family members—my grandmother, aunts, cousins—costs a fortune. My mother never complains. She just works harder. We never go without, at least not for long. We may spend a couple of winter nights without heat and we may have bread and butter sandwiches for dinner once in a while, but we shrug it off. *We'll get through this.* That's my mother's philosophy. She's right. We do. We more than survive. My mom always figures it out, with a smile on her face, and a song on her lips.

My mom has passed down her love of music to me. Music is her daily medicine, her fuel. She listens to the radio constantly. And she can sing. When nobody's around, especially when she's alone in the kitchen preparing a meal or cleaning up, she will turn up the radio and break into song, belting a gospel tune in a duet with Shirley Caesar or sing an R&B hit with Diana Ross and the Supremes, her voice soaring along to "Baby Love" or "You Can't Hurry Love." I think of her as the fourth Supreme. If Berry Gordy could hear her sing, I truly believe he would sign her up. She's that good.

My mother's friends greet me as they occupy the couch and the armchairs. They slide their drinks onto coasters on the coffee table and get comfortable. Within seconds, they turn their attention to me and the record I've got on.

Al Green.

My favorite singer.

A few weeks ago, Al Green released a new album, *I'm Still in Love with You.*

I've memorized every song.

The album is a wonder. Three of the songs—the title song, "Love and Happiness," and "Look What You Done for Me"—are number one hits and I love them all. But I am absolutely obsessed with one of the last songs on the second side of the album—"For the Good Times." I can listen to this song ten, twenty times in a row. And I have.

The thirty-five-second instrumental introduction to the song comes on now and I move my head to the soulful music. Of course, what I don't know then, at six years old, but will discover in my teens is that "For the Good Times" is a country song, written in 1968 by a famous Texas singer and songwriter, Kris Kristofferson. Two years later another Texan country singer, Ray Price, "the Cherokee Cowboy," covered the song, turning it into a country hit, Ray's twang enveloped in violins, his version sounding like a waltz. But now, in 1972, I know only that the song belongs to Al Green and I hear both country and Southern soul.

"Oh," one of the ladies says. "I love this song."

"Al Green," my mom says, catching my eye. "Did you know that we got a six-year-old Al Green right here?"

I don't know what gets into me, but prompted by my mom, I leap to my feet, duck into the kitchen, grab one of her fancy salt shakers, slide back into the living room in my stocking feet, and pretending the salt shaker is my mic, I begin singing along with Al Green, then *over* Al Green, lifting my voice, making the song my own.

"Don't look so sad—"

My mom's friends howl with surprise and joy.

I keep going, doing my best Al Green impression, crooning, *"Lay your head on my pillow—"*

"Sing it, Darius!" one of the ladies shouts.

Oh, I do. I do sing it. And I am *into* it. Overcome by it.

"I'll be here. I'm gonna stay right here—"

The ladies, my audience in their front row seats, love it. They stand, they dance, they clap, and then I go even further. I mimic Al Green, hitting his high notes, capturing his falsetto—

"Yeah, yeah, yeah . . . for the good times . . ."

I finish the song—all six and a half minutes—never letting my grip on Al Green go. I have captured his voice. I have captured his essence. I have co-opted his soul.

At least I believe I have.

And by the ovation I receive from my mom and her friends, they believe I have, too.

Beaming, I bow, clumsily, and then, feeling bold, even cocky with how well "For the Good Times" has gone over, I lean across the console, pick up the arm of the turntable, and place the needle on the first cut of the album, the title song, "I'm Still in Love with You." And when Al starts singing, I bring my salt shaker mic to my lips and I sing that song, too. What is it about Al Green that bores into my very being? It's more than his rhythm, his phrasing, his attitude. It's his actual—*voice.* I feel as if his honey-soaked voice has somehow entered me. *That's how I sound,* I think. *That's what I hear. I am Al Green.*

When "I'm Still in Love with You" finishes, and the next song starts, I sing that, and then Al and I launch into "Love and Happiness," and the next song, and the next, going hard on Al's raucous version of "Oh, Pretty Woman," reprising "For the Good Times," closing with the last song, "One of These Good Old Days."

I sing the entire album by heart.

I'm not sure at what point I completely lose myself in these songs, in this performance, in particular losing myself again in "For the Good Times," but I know I do. I'm so caught up in my singing that I'm not even here. I've entered some kind of zone. I'm completely lost in the performance of this music. And I know that these women, including my mother, are not merely indulging me. Far from it. As every good audience does, they become part of the performance. They're no longer my audience. They're my partners. We—my mom and her friends—share this hour of song. This music isn't mine; it's *ours*. Al Green's voice takes them higher, to a place they never knew they wanted to go, or could go. And I believe, with all my heart, that my voice propels them, my voice takes them there, to that place. My voice brings them there.

Something else happens, too.

I can't articulate it then, but I feel it. I know I have found it.

I am six years old and I have discovered *it*.

What I will do with my life.

As I stare at the salt shaker that fills up my small hand, my pretend mic, I know that someday, I will stand in front of a much larger audience, holding the real thing. Not a salt shaker. My own hand mic.

Singing.

My destiny.

3

"I WANT TO HOLD YOUR HAND"

The Beatles

I live in a compact, single-story house in an all-Black neighborhood in Charleston, on a street bordering the projects. I will spend my childhood through high school in that house. The house shakes with sound—folks talking, laughing, shouting, crying, my mother and grandmother laughing and singing while they cook and bake. The smells from meat and garlic crackling in frying pans, sauces simmering on the stove while bread dough rises, riding waves of heat from the oven, the scents rolling through the kitchen, reaching the far ends of the house, into the bedrooms, all these smells and voices, punctuated with music from the radio and hi-fi, our constant soundtrack. Always music. The house feels alive, a breathing being, a character itself with different personalities, never belonging to me alone.

My aunts—my mother's sisters—and their kids, my cousins, often crash with us. People entering, leaving, bodies everywhere. At times fifteen human beings share three bedrooms and one bathroom. The bathroom feels like a mini hotel lobby, with people coming in and out constantly. Folks frequently forget to lock the door. I'll step out of the shower and find one of my sisters or cousins brushing their teeth, or applying makeup, or even sitting on the toilet, oblivious to me as I frantically reach for a towel. The phone-booth-sized bathroom becomes emblematic of the house itself, a tiny rectangle where kids and adults negotiate, even fight, for an absolute minimum of space to maintain a semblance of basic hygiene. Today, whenever my kids complain about a lack of privacy, I laugh. *Privacy?* What is that? Growing up in my house, I never knew with whom I'd be sharing a bedroom and sometimes a bed—my younger brother, my cousin, my mother, my grand-mother.

Don't get me wrong. I *loved* my childhood. Those days informed me. I learned to achieve a kind of quiet equilibrium, to grasp and establish my own space amid chaos. I could have complained or acted out, but what would have been the point? Nothing would've changed. You either accepted the lack of privacy and other inconveniences or you'd go crazy. *Deal with it.* So, I did. Truth is, if I could enter a time machine and I had an opportunity to relive my life, I would choose the exact same childhood, all over again.

My mom is my hero. She approaches life with uncommon spirit and strength. She roars with laughter, her laugh huge and infectious. When she isn't laughing, she sings. She has a stunning voice, clear and strong and emotional, a voice that would fit seamlessly into any gospel choir. She sings along to any song that plays in our house, booming from the hi-fi in the living room or, when I get older, from my boom box, my prized possession, which my mother buys for me the year I turn eleven with money she earns working overtime. I close my eyes right now, drop my head, and after a moment, I evoke my mom's spirit. I can hear her voice. Sweet. Soaring. Rocking me. Lifting me.

Yes, music fills our house all the time, from the living room into the kitchen. I don't know quiet. We are a loud, boisterous, joyful house, punctuated by my mom's gospel music and R&B, and when I get old enough to take over the hi-fi by age five, my music. I put a record on the turntable or turn on the radio and listen to artists whose sounds fill most Black households in the early and mid-

1970s—Marvin Gaye singing all his early hits, especially "Let's Get It On," Gladys Knight & the Pips wailing "Midnight Train to Georgia," Stevie Wonder, Barry White, all their hits, songs that my mother sings to, her eyes closed, her body in slow, rhythmic time to the music. But as I get older, I go rogue and fill the house with music that I doubt you'd find in *any* Black household—KISS blasting "Rock and Roll All Nite," Cheap Trick pleading "I Want You to Want Me," Mick Jagger and the Rolling Stones screeching "Angie." Then I tune into a classic country station and turn up Buck Owens and his irresistible twang from the 1960s, crooning "Hello Trouble" and "I've Got a Tiger By the Tail." Then if I think my mother's out of earshot, I jump off the country music station and put on a Barry Manilow record. Yes. *Barry Manilow.* Give my mom props. She gets into Barry—a little. She even sings along to some of the songs. Well, maybe she tolerates the music because I love it so much. I really do love Barry—the crack and emotion of his voice, his dramatic lyrics—and I sing along to him, especially his song "Ships." My mom gives it her best shot, until she finally gives up and shouts into the living room, "Darius, turn off that Manilow, I can't take it anymore!" The rest of my family, give them credit, my sisters in particular, go along with my eclectic musical taste, except for KISS. They give me such shit about those Detroit rockers that they get physical. They attack me at the hi-fi, shoving me aside, blocking me so they can remove the KISS record and put on something else, anything else. My mother, though, takes my side, at least at first. She must sense something. She seems to know that my musical obsession—even about KISS—is more than a phase.

"You leave him alone," she shouts. "Let him listen to whatever he wants."

I grin at my mother, my protector, and glare at my sisters and cousins, my tormentors, and then I triumphantly play the next KISS cut on the album *Detroit Rock City.* I move to the beat and nod to the jangling, head-banging guitar playing, and then I begin singing along to Paul Stanley. My mother hangs in there with me for about twenty seconds, her forehead furrowed in either fierce concentration or intense pain. Finally, she leans over the hi-fi and says with a grimace, "Darius, honey, I can't. I just can't. I love you but I *can't*." Then, without looking at my cousins, my sisters, or me, she shuts down KISS, slides the record off the turntable, and with a sigh of relief, puts on Al Green.

One day, rummaging in the drawer beneath the hi-fi, I come upon two 45s I hadn't seen before—"I Want to Hold Your Hand" and "She Loves You" by The Beatles. I'm not sure who bought these records—one of my sisters, or maybe my older brother, Ricky, but I can't wait to play them. I put them on the hi-fi, drop the needle on one, then the other, and then I play them both again, and then flip them over and play the B-sides, "This Boy" and "I'll Get You," again, and again—for an hour, or two, I can't tell. Time evaporates. I'm completely transported, lost in this music. The music enters me like an infusion. It pulsates through me. I can't listen to The Beatles enough. Another hour passes. Then another. Not only am I not sick of these songs, of these voices, the melodies, the harmonies, I want more. Thus begins a lifelong obsession—and fascination—with The Beatles.

What is it about a song? I think. What is it about a song that connects to me so deeply? The lyrics? The melody? The beat? The singer's voice?

All of it. All those things.

And one more thing.

The key thing.

When a song finishes, I want to hear it again.

That's the defining thing.

I want to hear the song again. No. I *have* to hear it again.

Not just once. Over and over. Repeatedly. Dozens and dozens of times. I listen to a song I love not for hours, but for *days*.

I listen until the song inserts itself into me, until it becomes a part of my soul.

. . .

In *To Kill a Mockingbird*, Harper Lee writes that you can choose your friends, but you can't choose your family.

I have an incredibly tight group of friends. We are ridiculously close. We are thrown together by circumstance, but then we choose each other, friends for life.

We are babies when we meet, all of us in diapers, living in the same neighborhood, a few houses apart. I am six months old when I meet two of the guys and a year and a half when I meet the others. Our moms or grandmothers or aunts or older sisters babysit us. We learn to walk and talk together. We grow up together, from babies and toddlers through elementary school, junior high, and high school. We become inseparable and remain close to this day. Our secret? We're into having as much fun as possible, at all times. And we *share*. Thoughts. Feelings. Very un-guy like. No subject is off-limits. The six of us can ask for anything, anytime. It is honestly easier for me to be friends with these guys than to be friends with myself.

The group:

Sheldon Simmons.

We call him Glob.

One day, in high school, we sneak beers for lunch. Lazing in the cafeteria, probably tipsy, Sheldon says, "I got no dick, got no balls, just got one big glob."

So, from then on—Glob.

David Campbell.

He goes by Squirt.

Rick Johannes.

The only white guy in our group.

We call him White Boy Rick. Obviously.

Sheldon Snipe.

No nickname.

Yes. We have two Sheldons. We call this one Sheldon Snipe to avoid confusion with Glob.

Juan Ferguson.

He's Juan. Just Juan.

I love my family. I'm close with my sisters and my brother, Jamar. But in many ways, I'm even closer with these guys. We actually bleed together, more than once. Playing superheroes, my cape a towel tied around my shoulders, I, a five-year-old Superman, launch myself off Snipe's front porch, expecting—what—to fly? I land chin-first on the concrete sidewalk. Blood gushes from my split and mangled chin. Screams, chaos. Then I'm in the back seat of the Snipe family's car, my towel-cape now pressed against my chin, soaked in blood, Snipe's sister driving me to the ER at the hospital where my mother works. She stops at a stop sign and sees my mom on the other side, driving home. Snipe's sister waves, we frantically switch cars, and my mom turns around, heading back to the ER. After that I remember my mom handing me off to the staff at the ER, leaning over me, smiling reassuringly: "You'll be fine. I'm gonna go hang out with my friends."

Our group of six. Brothers. Closer than brothers. Certainly closer than I am or ever will be to my brother Ricky.

. . .

I am the youngest of five children. I assume I always will be. I'm counting on it. Being the baby comes with perks. Mom and I have a special bond, with my being her youngest little boy. And then, when I'm eleven, Jamar shows up. My new little brother. What an unexpected bundle of joy. Yeah. Right. Now Mom gives all her attention to this needy, squawking infant. Suddenly, I'm no longer her baby—he is. Kind of pisses me off.

I get over it quickly. Got no choice. Mom goes back to work as soon as she can because she has to. The rest of us kids, me and my three sisters, take over running the house, which includes caring for Jamar. We operate well together, despite or maybe because of our differences.

Before me comes Bonnie, two years older. We're fighters, the two of us, against everyone else and sometimes against each other. Bonnie's an athlete, a basketball star, and she will take you on. We go at each other hard. She's a girl, which means nothing. She's a powerhouse. She plays sports like a guy, and she punches like a guy. Trust me.

Before Bonnie, a year older, comes Valerie. Val is petite and quiet. Val has a huge heart and an ocean-sized amount of patience. She doesn't say much, but when she does, she speaks with wisdom and care. I can always count on Val—to talk to, to hear me out, especially when Mom is at work, or when she's so tired from working that she collapses on the couch right after dinner.

L'Corine—French for "beautiful maiden"—is my oldest sister, a year older than Val. L'Corine was born with a high-octane engine roaring inside her. She *moves*. Always in motion. She's Mom 2.0, assertive, motivated, a go-getter. When Mom's not at home, L'Corine takes over. No-nonsense. The boss. L'Corine is in charge.

I ease into my role with them. It's not hard. We connect, all of us, in different ways, and we always figure it out. We work well together, parceling out the chores, sharing the responsibilities. We make the family work. I love them all.

And then there's Ricky.

The oldest sibling.

My older brother. Seven years older.

Rail thin. Hyper. On edge. Frenetic.

Ricky is an epileptic, prone to seizures.

His seizures ruin my mom. I get that she has to care for him when the seizures come, but she babies him before, during, and after. The way I see it, she always gives Ricky whatever he wants. Money's tight, but she manages to give in to him, finding something extra, in her purse, in a pocket, in a drawer. He asks, she gives. Ricky is not helpless. Not at all. Despite his epilepsy, he's a good athlete. He's smart as a whip, too.

He also bullies me, terrorizes me, belittles me.

Ricky never gives anything to anyone, not to me, our sisters, nobody. Ricky only takes. Our family has very little to give. He doesn't care. He takes whatever he can, whatever he sees, whatever he can get his hands on, whether it belongs to him or not. Ricky gets into drugs. I'm eleven and I don't know what Ricky's using, but I know Ricky can't hold a job. He has offers. Boeing recruits him. They come after him, invite him to a six-month training program in Seattle. The morning he's supposed to leave for Seattle, he refuses to get out of bed. He decides he's not going. Too far. Too much trouble. He's not into it. The excuses fly out of his mouth like darts. He'd rather stay here, live off Mom and my sisters, be responsible to no one, hit the streets, get high, get beaten up, which happens frequently, and end up in the hospital or in jail, which happens constantly.

"Where's Ricky?" we ask.

He's high again. He got beat up again. No, he's in jail again.

We breathe a sigh of relief. We feel safer. A least he's not on the streets getting the shit kicked out of him, or doing drugs, passed out in some doorway. Or, honestly, at home, where Ricky's neediness takes over every inch of space in the house. As soon as he walks into a room, you feel stifled. Ricky sucks the air and energy out of every room he enters. He's a human Hoover.

"He can't help himself," my mother says.

I wonder. I'm eleven but I'm not sure what she says is right. On some level, I understand. And I do sympathize. He's her firstborn, her first son, and watching Ricky self-destruct day after day must be destroying her. He can't figure anything out. He can't figure himself out.

But I feel that Ricky takes advantage of my mom's loving heart and generous spirit, and he uses her. I believe he *can* help himself. He could have worked for Boeing, begun a career, made his own money, become—*something.* But no, he just takes and takes and takes, knowing that my mom—and my sisters—will always be there for him, enabling him, providing for him, taking care of him, no matter how many times he gets high on the streets, gets the crap kicked out of him, or lands in jail.

. . .

My boom box becomes an appendage of my arm, attached to my head and shoulders. I keep it with me always. I put it down only to change cassettes. I bring it with me everywhere. At night, because I know Ricky, I bring my boom box to bed with me. I would never leave it within ten feet of Ricky. I know he'll steal it, bring it out on the streets, and sell it for money to buy drugs, any drugs. He's that addicted and that desperate. So, I sleep with my boom box. Every night.

Except one night I forget.

I come home from hanging with my guys and I leave my boom box on the dining room table.

I wake up the next morning, feel for my boom box in my bed, remember where I left it, bolt out of bed, burst out of my room in my pajamas, sprint into the dining room, and skid to a stop in front of the dining room table.

The bare dining room table.

My boom box is gone.

Later, when Ricky wakes up, I confront him.

I tell him I know that he took my boom box.

He makes a dismissive sound and turns away from me.

I don't let up. I tell him I *know* he took my boom box. I'm seven years younger but I get into his face.

He screams at me. Swears he never saw my boom box.

I tell him I know he's lying. He screams at me again. Comes at me.

My mother intervenes. My sisters appear. They all know what happened. They know Ricky stole my boom box.

I fight back tears. I will not cry. I won't give him that satisfaction.

He denies he stole my boom box—he lies again—and then he storms off, indignant, as if he's the victim.

I look at my mom and my sisters. They know the truth. But what can they do? I really don't know. I feel helpless. I suppose it's my fault for leaving my boom box on the dining room table, in plain sight of Ricky.

The next day arrives like any other day. School, homework, hanging with my friends. Small talk around the dinner table. Nobody mentions the boom box. It's like it never existed. I say nothing to Ricky. I don't want to speak to him. But my mother talks to him as if nothing has happened. Like everything else in this house, I think, it's all about Ricky. Always about Ricky. I look over at him, at my older brother, and I can almost hear my mom's thoughts.

At least he's not having a seizure. At least he's not on the streets. At least he's not in the hospital. At least he's not in jail.

. . .

Once I get to college, I find myself wanting to stay away from home, mainly because I don't want to deal with Ricky, his neediness, his drug abuse, his constant begging for money. When I do come home, he no longer bullies me. He can't. I'm bigger, stronger, and he knows if he pushes me, I'll kick the crap out of him. Instead, he looks at me like I'm an ATM. Press my buttons and I'll hand him some cash. I do. I admit it. But only for a while.

Years later, as I predict, my good-hearted sister L'Corine takes him in. Her husband, Marvin, a saint, puts up with him, but I can see that Ricky is taking a toll on them both. I can't stand to see Ricky manipulating my sister for a place to live, and for money to live on. At one point, I hit the road with the band. I keep track of my siblings from the road. Ricky's manipulations anger me. He still uses, he still ends up in the hospital, he still ends up in jail. I can hear my mother's voice. *What can you do? Poor Ricky.*

A few years later, I have Thanksgiving at my house. My career has gone well, but I've had several knee operations. After a while, my knees finally work like normal knees following a series of painful recoveries. Agonizing, debilitating pain. Needed pills to get me through.

For the holiday, I have the whole family over. Aunts, uncles, cousins. Everyone. Including Ricky. The next morning, bleary-eyed, hungover from too much turkey and too many shots of bourbon, I open a drawer in my bathroom cabinet to get some aspirin, and I immediately know something is off. Usually when I open the drawer, I hear the rattle of the bottle of leftover Oxy pills I keep inside. This time, no rattle. I pick up the bottle and see that it's empty.

Ricky.

He's stolen the Oxy.

I remember that I have other bottles of Oxy lying around, unused, no longer needed.

I find the bottles.

All empty.

Ricky has stolen all of the Oxy in the house.

I am pissed, not just at him, but at myself for being so careless. But the anger at myself passes. *Ricky. I've cut you so much slack. Given you so much. Including money. Even more than that. Time and time again I've given you my attention. My energy. My concern. My worry.*

I know he can't help himself, but as long as he lives with my sister and Marvin, I think, Ricky will always just *take* and my other sisters and I will always enable him.

Until now.

This moment.

This morning after Thanksgiving.

The last straw.

For my own mental health, I decide to let him go. Fend for himself. I will accept whatever happens. I decide to keep my distance from him. I refuse to allow him to squeeze me dry anymore—mentally, emotionally, financially. He's a grown man. He has to start acting like one.

Except I know in my heart that he can't.

One night, smashed, fucked up, a seizure coming on, Ricky falls, hits his head, and bleeds to death.

I feel overcome by sadness. But I also feel relief. Ricky's sad, repetitive loop of a life wasted has come to its inevitable end.

I think of my mother. I see her sitting in the living room, her head down, her shoulders heaving, sobbing because Ricky, once again, is in jail. I imagine her voice wailing through her tears. "I don't know what to do. What can I do?"

Even at age eleven, I remember thinking during one of those nights—those many nights when Ricky was locked up—I will never do that to her. I will never make her cry like that. I will make something of myself. I will make her proud of me.

So, maybe, in some way, Ricky did serve a purpose for me.

Motivation.

A reason to succeed.

To be nothing like him.

Ricky.

Poor Ricky.

All he wanted was to get high.

All I wanted was an older brother.

4

"SHIPS"

Barry Manilow

*W*e walked to the sea, just my father and me . . .
We're two ships that pass in the night.
I am six years old.

Saturday morning. I'm dressed and eating breakfast, a bowl of cereal, before eight o'clock. I finish breakfast, stand on a stool in front of the sink, wash my dishes, dry them, and put them away. I check the kitchen clock. Eight-fifteen. I'm nervous. But also excited. My dad will be here at nine to pick me up. We're going out for the day. I haven't seen him for a year or more. We're not really in touch. He never visits me. But Mom told me he's coming today. Going to have a day together, just the two of us. She looks skeptical when she tells me. In her eyes, I read, *I'll believe he's coming when I see it.* I'm too excited to doubt her. Too blind, too young, too naive to doubt him.

My dad doesn't arrive at nine. Or ten. Or noon. He doesn't come all afternoon. Then around five o'clock, while I'm on the living room floor listening to the hi-fi, I hear a truck rumbling up our street and stopping in front of our house and I hear voices outside. I fling the front door open and I see my dad standing on the street, directing two guys who are hauling a pool table off the bed of a pickup truck. He sees me and waves.

"Got detained," he says. "But look at this."

"A pool table?"

He grins. "For you."

He turns back to the guys, grabs a side of the pool table, and leads them into the house.

"What's this?" my mother shouts from the edge of the living room.

"What's it look like?"

"Oh, no. *No*." My mother tries to stop the guys from bringing the pool table inside, but my father pushes past her. He and the guys place the pool table in a corner of the living room. The guys, their heads lowered, brush by my mother and me and leave. My father—everyone calls him Blue—stands tall and grins at her.

"You can't leave that here," my mother says.

"Carolyn, please, it's a gift."

"Where did you get it?"

"Don't worry about it. It's hardly used."

My father bends down so we're eye to eye.

"You like it?"

I nod.

I want to tell my father that I waited all day to see him. I've been waiting to see him for over a year. I want to tell him that a pool table doesn't matter. *He* matters. Seeing him—hanging out with him—matters. He is the only thing that matters to me.

"I like a good game of pool," my father says.

He rubs my head and stands up. "Well, I got to go."

And then my father leaves.

He flies out the front door, scrabbles down the stairs, and disappears into the night, as if he'd never been here, as if this past ten minutes had been a dream, nothing but a dream.

I see him again a year later. And then again a year after that. I see him once a year for a few years in a row. Then I don't see him again for fifteen years.

But for the next three years after he brings me the pool table, all I do is play pool. I am determined to get good at pool. I become laser-focused on the game. I practice every chance I get. It pays off. I become a nine-year-old pool shark.

Dad, I know you like a good game of pool. I'm ready now. I'm good at pool.

If I get good at pool, maybe my father will want to be with me.

. . .

I hear his voice.

We go to church every Sunday morning. We never miss. My grandmother Rose, who lives with us, insists that we attend and we participate and we pray. Every week, we go to St. John Baptist Church, a twenty-minute drive from our house. I'm in elementary school, nine years old, and I don't love getting out of bed first thing Sunday morning to spend three hours in church, bored and restless in wooden pews. I don't jump out of bed, get into my Sunday clothes, and rush happily into the car. I take my time. I move slowly. I linger. Sometimes I mope. But there's no way around it. *You will go to church.* No questions asked.

But once I'm there, I get caught up in the music. The piano. Tambourine. The passion of the choir. The voices. The clapping. The rhythm. The shouting. I may have taken my sweet time leaving the house, but I forget about that now. I'm nine years old and at church, I find the music. Those gospel songs. The hymns. The sweet soul music, especially "It Is Well with My Soul." The music pulls me out of that wooden pew, lifts me up, and takes me away. Come for the Lord. The community. The prayers. The preaching. The sermon. But stay for the music. Once again, the music.

One Sunday morning, as we drive to church, my mother tunes the radio to WPAL, the local R&B station. Sunday mornings, the station plays live gospel music. This morning, a local gospel group calling themselves The Rolling Stones—later changing their name to the Traveling Echoes—comes on. As the harmonies of their voices cascade and intertwine, my mother turns up the volume.

"You hear that tenor?" my mother says.

The tenor. The honey-soaked, higher-pitched voice, caressing the melody, rising above the others.

"Yes."

"That's your dad."

I say nothing. I'm too shocked to speak.

I never see my dad. He doesn't come around, doesn't visit me, doesn't call me. He has cut me out of his life. But now every Sunday morning, driving to church, I hear his voice, his tenor soaring in a gospel song, live, praising the Lord.

Take my hand, precious Lord.

Lead me home.

I hear him in the car. I lean in and listen to his voice.

It's all I have of him.

5

"LOVE'S IN NEED OF LOVE TODAY"

Stevie Wonder

I'm ten years old and my life is all about music.

With one exception.

Football.

I love sports, but I live for football.

I have found my game, my passion, my reason. I love to sing and spend hours listening to music, but I become obsessed about football. I dream about playing in the NFL. I see myself as a star quarterback, zipping passes to my wide receivers and running on my own for first downs and touchdowns, slithering through a maze of tacklers and then speeding past the rest of the defense into the end zone.

My friends and I meet for pickup games at our small local park and in the fall we join Pop Warner. We play ten games a season and I do play quarterback. I excel and our team makes the play-offs. At night, I lie in bed, replaying the most recent game in my head, watching a personal highlights film. Next to me, I cradle my football, fearful that if I leave it anywhere else in the house, Ricky will snatch it and sell it. I fall asleep with the cool cowhide tucked against my cheek.

Our team roars through the playoffs, making it to the championship game. We lose a squeaker, but I've played my heart out and we've had a great season. The team forms our final huddle, our arms around each other. We break, and as we begin to pick up our gear, our coach reminds us that we'll all be together one last time, at the season's culmination, the father-son banquet.

The words sting.

All of us will be together, one last time.

Everyone except me.

I won't be able to attend the father-son banquet.

I don't have a father to take me.

I slowly gather my helmet, jacket, and my cherished football. I glance across the field and see the other kids leaving the park, many with their dads. The last to leave, the lone straggler, I say goodbye to our coach. I offer him my hand to shake because I know I won't see him for a while, at least until the start of the next season. As for the trophy I'm supposed to receive at the father-son banquet, I guess I'll pick that up some other time. My coach and I shake hands, awkwardly. As I leave the park, I can feel him watching me. I wonder if he knows I won't be attending the father-son banquet.

Of course he knows. We play our games in a small neighborhood park. The kids know each other. The parents know each other. The coaches know each other. Everybody knows everyone and everybody knows everything that's going on. Sometimes I feel as if I live in a fishbowl. And sometimes, like when I think about the father-son banquet and that I won't be able to go and everyone in the world knows why, I wish I could disappear.

The night of the banquet, I mope around the house, throw on some sweats, and settle on the couch to watch TV. Before I'm comfortable, I hear a knock at the front door. I open the door and find Mr. Campbell, Squirt's dad, who's also a coach in our league, standing there. He's wearing a sport coat and slacks. He rubs his palm over his slick, bald head and pats his wondrous, thick mustache.

"You ready?" he says.

"Huh?"

"Come on. We got to get a move on."

I start to stammer. "What are you—where are we going?"

"The father-son banquet. Get dressed. You got five minutes."

I don't remember much more of that evening. I remember getting dressed and going to the banquet and sitting at a round table with Mr. Campbell, my surrogate dad, and seeing him smile and applaud along with the rest of the fathers and sons as our coach presents me my trophy.

Later, when Mr. Campbell drops me off and I thank him for taking me to the banquet, I go into my house, close the door to my room, and I make a decision. My dad has chosen to remove himself from my life. I don't have any say in that. But I do have a say in how to respond to that in the future. I decide I will no longer wait for him, ever. I decide to let him go. He can live his own life, and I will live mine.

. . .

I don't have a dad. I feel weirdly singled out, wondering if people are looking at me, feeling sorry for me. Thankfully, crazily, wonderfully, I inherit five other dads. My friends' dads. All of them, each in his own way, becomes a surrogate father to me.

Mr. Campbell becomes a major father figure. Rugged-looking and tough on the outside, he reminds me of a former football player. He always gives me his full attention and then hears me out, allowing me to express myself. When he offers advice, he speaks with care and kindness. He also takes no crap and calls us out—Squirt and me and all of us—if we get in trouble in school or at home, and especially if we talk trash in front of him.

"D, are you talking trash to me?" he says. "I will wrestle you right now. Let's go."

That shuts me up. Shuts us all up. Believe me, the last thing you want to do is wrestle Mr. Campbell.

. . .

I get into a fight at school and the principal suspends me for a day. I retreat to my room and lose myself in my music. My sister Bonnie bangs on my door and barges into my room. She punches her fists onto her hips and speaks with a snotty you-are-in-so-much-trouble expression on her face. "Mr. Campbell's here."

"Why?"

"Oh, I don't know. Maybe because he wants to *see* you. He doesn't look happy."

I find Mr. Campbell waiting for me on the porch. He gestures for me to sit across from him. Bonnie's right. He doesn't look happy.

"I heard what happened at school," he says.

"How do you know—?"

I stop myself. Of course Mr. Campbell would know. He's a coach and he knows everyone. Everyone knows everyone and everything.

"You talk trash, you get into a fight, and you get suspended. *Not acceptable.*"

He speaks low and drags those two words out for about ten ominous seconds each.

I hang my head.

I have disappointed Squirt's Dad. It somehow feels worse than if I had disappointed my own dad.

"You are not too old for me to beat your ass," Mr. Campbell says. "Because if I don't, when your mom gets home from work, you know that she will."

I keep my focus on the porch floor.

"Darius, look at me."

I raise my head, meet his narrowed eyes.

"This is your last warning. Am I clear?"

"Yes, Mr. Campbell, crystal clear."

After that, I change my behavior at school. I hold my tongue and watch my step. As I say, you do not want to wrestle with Mr. Campbell.

When I turn fourteen, I start spending more and more time with my friend Rick Johannes and soon we become inseparable. I ride my bike to his house, a few blocks away, and we either play sports or just hang out. I introduce him to my current musical obsession—Stevie Wonder, especially his new album, *Songs in the Key of Life,* two CDs and almost two hours of stunning songs. We can barely get past the leadoff song, "Love's in Need of Love Today," listening to it alone for an hour, and then "Sir Duke" and "I Wish" bring us to our feet, dancing and strutting across his room like we're featured dancers on *Soul Train.* Yes, me and White Boy Rick.

I find myself spending more time at Rick's house than at home. I practically live there. I go there after school, on weekends, I stay for dinner. I become a de facto member of the Johannes family. I feel so welcome at Rick's house that I don't want to leave. Rick's dad, a captain in the navy, makes sure to include me in everything he and Rick do. And sometimes, Captain Johannes—or Captain Dick—takes me aside and talks to me about my life and my future.

"Darius, what do you think you might want to do after high school? Have you thought about a career? Do you have a plan? Have you thought about college?"

"Not really."

"It's not that far off. Four years. That's nothing. Time has a way of sneaking up on you. We can talk about it. Anytime you want. Just remember, you can do anything. Never say no to yourself."

"Thanks."

My plan? My future? A career? Sports, I think. If I don't make it to the NFL, I see myself as a sports journalist, a broadcaster.

Yes. My future is in sports.

. . .

One day, Captain Dick comes into Rick's room, where we're hanging out.

"Hey, Rick, get dressed, we're going to go play golf."

Mr. Johannes starts to leave, then stops and says, "Darius, you want to go?"

I have never played golf, don't know how to play, but I say, "Absolutely."

"Good. Rick will set you up."

I borrow some of Rick's clothes, which he says you have to wear when you play golf. It turns out that playing golf requires a certain dress code, including special shoes, with cleats. Rick has his own set of clubs so I borrow his mom's clubs. Practically new. She's happy to lend them to me.

We play at a nearby air force golf course. We politely wait our turn to tee off and we talk low, in whispers. Golf seems so civilized, almost formal, with strict rules that you have to follow before, during, and after you hit each shot. It almost feels like you're in the military. No wonder Captain Johannes loves the game so much. I watch him and Rick hit their tee shots and then I step onto the flat mound of grass to hit my first golf shot ever. As they've instructed, I step up to the ball, keep my head down, swing, follow through, and—surprise—I connect. *Thwack.* The flat wooden surface of the driver whips through in an arc and my ball blasts off like a missile. Rick and his dad shout and clap. I stand riveted on the tee, watching my ball fly on a line into the blue sky.

"Wow," I say.

I don't say that about the shot. I say that about what I feel. I feel something deep and powerful and almost overwhelming. A sense of amazement and joy courses through me, followed by something else. Another strong, even stranger feeling.

Love.

That's it.

I'm fourteen and I have fallen in love—

With a game. With the setting. The rules. All of it.

It happens instantly, in less than a second. I stand on the tee, my eyes fastened on the ball, soaring into the sky. I watch the ball land on the manicured green fairway and then roll, and keep on rolling until it comes to a stop somewhere on the horizon.

Yes. Love.

Love at first flight, I think.

I hit other spectacular shots that day. I even make a par or two. Of course, I also hit dozens of other shots that suck. I duff shots and shank drives, and whack several short putts too hard, staring unbelievably at the ball skittering past the pin. My emotions range from unbearably frustrated to ridiculously overjoyed. All of it, thrilling.

On the third hole, as Rick lines up his putt, I pull the flag out of the cup and drop it on the green, causing the flag to slap on the ground, hard.

Captain Johannes comes over to me and places his hand on my shoulder.

"Son, that's not how we do it. You take out the flag, and you place it down, gently, out of the way. You can't do that jarring move. You don't want to mess with people's lines."

I nod, thank him, making sure from then on that I take care of the flag carefully. I tend the flag that way to this day. But Rick's dad taught me more than how to tend the flag. He taught me to respect the game.

I start playing regularly with Rick and Captain Johannes. The second or third time we play, Rick's dad hands me Mrs. Johannes's clubs. He watches me sling the bag over my shoulder as we head toward the car.

"How do you feel about those clubs?" Captain Johannes asks.

"Oh, I love them."

"They're yours."

For a moment, I can't speak.

"Mrs. Johannes doesn't really play. She told me to give them to you."

"Are you sure?"

"Definitely."

I thank him and later I thank Mrs. Johannes. Those clubs. My first set. A perfect fit. I play with those clubs for the next ten years.

6

"WALK ON THE WILD SIDE"

Lou Reed

When I'm in elementary school, I go to church because I have to. By the time I hit my teens, I go because I want to. Not that I have a choice. But I actually look forward to Sunday mornings. As I said before, I'm into church for the music. When the choir revs up and gets into it, opening their voices wide and letting themselves go, I'm on my feet along with everyone else, clapping, swaying, singing along. The choir numbers fifty or so and their voices lift the roof off that building. The singing, shouting, clapping, dancing—the sanctuary swells with joyful sound. But it's even more than music. It's a performance—for God. Spiritual. Dramatic. Histrionic. The Sunday morning music moves me, makes me deliriously happy. This church music stirs my soul.

Some people in my family think that I should listen only to this music. Spiritual music. Church music. Or if not church music alone, Black music. They have become indoctrinated into their own community and the Black church and they believe I should become indoctrinated, too. They believe I should not listen to Led Zeppelin. Or R.E.M. Or KISS. Or Lou Reed and the Velvet Underground. And I should definitely not tune into *Hee Haw*, hosted by country singers Roy Clark and Buck Owens, every Saturday night.

I do anyway. I not only listen to this music and watch *Hee Haw*, I love it.

I don't see the problem. It's music. Notes. Words. Maybe some different-sounding voices. But still music. You have the same notes and same words no matter what music you listen to. Thank God for my mom. My sisters and brothers hate Lou Reed and KISS.

"Like fingernails on a chalkboard," one of them says. "My head's gonna explode. Turn it off."

But my mother takes my side. She lets me listen to anything I want, at least for a while, until the music becomes too grating for her, too. She doesn't get Lou Reed at all. She and my siblings just don't hear music the way I do. They can't hear it. They don't even consider the stuff I listen to *music*. But I get Lou Reed's nasally, atonal speak-singing. He doesn't sound like anybody else. He has a one-of-a-kind voice and point of view. It's personal, almost primitive, but so smart and defiant, describing a world that's dangerous, dark, edgy. His world. To me, his *New York* album is a rap record. I listen to Lou Reed over and over and I hear something new and fresh each time. Not sure I would want to visit his New York in real life, but I love visiting through his words and music.

. . .

I turn fifteen and enter sophomore year of high school. Four of my close group of friends—Squirt, Glob, Snipe, Juan—and I walk together in a pack to our school, Middleton High in Charleston. The walk from our neighborhood to the high school covers a good mile. We take our time, partly because we're in no hurry to get to school, but mostly because our backpacks weigh a ton and lugging them over this mile route slows us down and kills our backs. We walk hunched over, five human question marks. I feel as if I'm in marine basic training on a forced march.

We begin in our neighborhood, predominately Black and mostly poor, then after a while, maybe a half mile in, we walk through a white neighborhood. As we trudge our way through this cluster of bigger homes, larger front lawns, and wider streets, a school bus pulls up to a corner in front of us and stops. The doors hiss open and a steady flow of white high school kids, laughing, shouting, jostling each other, climbs into the bus. A few minutes later, with the last student settled inside, the doors snap shut, and the bus pulls away, carrying this group of white kids—our classmates—to Middleton.

"I wonder why they get a bus in their neighborhood and we don't?" Squirt says.

"Yeah," I say. "I wonder."

We keep going, walking slowly, our backpacks threatening to tip us over, slogging the rest of the way to school, still a half mile to go, refusing to speak about the blatant yet quiet racism we've just witnessed, but all of us thinking, No bus is ever gonna come to our neighborhood, the Black neighborhood. We're never riding a bus.

So, there it is.

In Black and white.

Racism.

Obvious or subtle, expressed in a shout or a whisper.

Doesn't matter. It's still racism.

. . .

I do well in high school. I make a lot of friends across a spectrum of social circles and I'm voted vice president of the senior class. I get bored and antsy in the classroom, but I keep busy after school. I participate in the glee club, join the Key Club and Big Brothers Big Sisters.

Mostly, though, I sing. I sing because I want to and I can. It's what I do. Who I am. Since the age of six, my voice has simply been a part of me, as real and as natural as my breath. I have no training, take no classes, I just know I can sing. Like a fast runner gifted with speed, I, too, have been blessed with a gift. I accept my gift, embrace it. And so, I sing. I become a member of the Middleton Singers, our fifty-voice show choir. We travel to other schools and I make my mark, singing several leads. Then as the fall semester comes to an end, I get serious about college.

I know I want to go to a college with a Division 1 football program. I want the traditional college experience. Big green campus. Tons of students. Lots of choices, opportunities. And I want football every Saturday, including tailgating before each game and partying afterward. I have given up my dream of playing in the NFL, but I have not lost my love of football. I send away for a dozen college catalogs and after they arrive, I spread them all out on the kitchen table. My mom and I glance from one glossy college scene on each catalog cover to the next.

"This is confusing," she says.

"Not really," I say.

Because I've already made my choice. I know which college I want to attend.

I'd recently read an article in *Playboy* written by humorist Erma Bombeck in which she listed the top twenty-five party schools in the country. After going through all twenty-five, Erma ended the article by writing, "You're probably wondering why I didn't mention the University of South Carolina. That's because I don't mix professionals with amateurs."

Sold.

"Mom," I say, handing her the catalog for the University of South Carolina. "I'm going here."

She looks at me, then brushes her palm over the front of the catalog. "I just want you to be happy."

. . .

First semester freshman year at the University of South Carolina.

I'm not happy.

I'm miserable.

Classic case of freshman blues. I feel out of place, lost, bordering on depressed.

Except for attending class, studying in the library, and going to football games on Saturdays, I stay in my room. I don't really do anything else. I can't find a social circle. I'm overwhelmed by the size of this school. I've gone from smallish Middleton High, where I knew practically everyone, to a college of thirty thousand students where I know basically no one. As time goes on, my loneliness gets worse. I can't motivate myself to meet people or go to parties. I have become isolated, essentially a hermit. I keep holed up in my nondescript dorm room in Moore Residence Hall, a concrete rectangular box that feels more like a prison than a college residence hall. I am so unhappy that I decide to transfer.

"I made a mistake," I tell my mom over Thanksgiving. "I have to get out of there."

As always, she supports me unconditionally and even helps me choose another college. We narrow the choices down to two and then I go back to South Carolina to finish my freshman year.

I remain a recluse until about ten days before the end of first semester.

One night, I take a break from studying and attend a hall meeting in the lounge on our dorm floor. As the meeting ends and everyone gets up to leave, I hear three words that will change my life.

"Where you going?"

I look up and see a guy about my size, a little taller maybe, grinning at me, his smile wide enough to light up the room. I don't know him but I've seen him around. He's a presence, friendly, social, always hitting people up with his high-beam smile. He reminds me of a good-looking Jim Varney.

"I'm just going back to my room to study," I say.

"Well, when you're done or you want to take a break, come over to my room. Couple of guys are gonna drop by. We're gonna hang out, have a few beers. Join us."

"Okay, sure," I say, completely thrown by the invitation.

"I'm Chris," the guy says, as we shake hands. "Chris Carney."

"Darius," I say.

I go back to my room, sit at my desk, and open my textbook, intending to study for an hour or so. After five minutes, I close the book. I can't go to Chris's room yet. Don't want to seem too eager. Or desperate. I wait five more minutes.

I knock on Chris Carney's door. He opens up, grins, and slaps a beer into my palm. I enter his room and he enters my life, forever.

. . .

Carney and I spend the final ten days of first semester freshman year together, practically glued to each other's side. Chris's room becomes party central. Kids come and go, beer flows, music blasts, and laughter—mine, Carney's, everyone's—shakes the room continuously. I know I'm making up for months of lost time, but I can't remember a period of more sheer, crazy *fun*. At South Carolina, home of the party professionals, I have come alive. Shortly, I give up my amateur status and become a party pro. Just like Erma Bombeck said. Finally.

After those ten days, everything changes.

I go home for winter break, inform my mom that I've decided not to transfer after all, and I return to South Carolina for second semester—early. I arrive well before Moore Hall officially opens. I stand outside the closed doors of the dormitory with my suitcase, waiting. I look left and I see another kid arriving with his suitcase, also early, also eager to get the party started.

Carney.

We make eye contact, shrug, and crack up.

. . .

I believe in destiny.

Fifteen people attended the meeting in the student lounge that night at the end of my first semester freshman year. Why did Carney pick me out? What was it that made him say, "Where you going?" and invite me to his room for a drink?

If Carney doesn't do that, I transfer out of South Carolina and go to another school.

And Hootie & The Blowfish doesn't exist.

7

"HONESTY"

Billy Joel

Nineteen eighty-five.

Sophomore year.

I have joined Carolina Alive, the campus show choir. We're sort of a big deal. We perform during halftime at basketball games and at a ton of other campus events. We go on road trips, too, to other schools, community centers, senior citizen homes, even to the statehouse. On some of the songs, the director features me. I score two big leads, one, remarkably, at President Reagan's second inauguration. The other one's even better. At a local arena, the show choir backs up the rock band Foreigner on their hit "I Want to Know What Love Is" and I sing with Lou Gramm, the band's lead singer. For me, this moment lands somewhere between a dream and an out-of-body experience.

One day, an early Thursday afternoon in late September, I head down the hall to the showers on our dorm floor. I'm looking forward to taking a shower for two reasons. First, Carney and I are going out tonight. We'll be drinking for sure, and as a bonus attraction, he knows a guy who might be willing to sell us a couple sheets of acid.

Second, nobody is around and I can sing at the top of my lungs. Moore Hall is a drab dorm with prison showers—several showers in a row—but the acoustics are superb. You get a clear, crisp, honey-soaked sound that bounces off the tile, amplifying you, bathing you in your own voice.

I choose the perfect shower song, "Honesty" by Billy Joel. I sing every note, every word. I belt the song like I'm Billy Joel himself, letting loose on an arena stage in front of fifty thousand people. I sing the entire song and then I sing it *again*.

Finished showering, I dry off, wrap a towel around my waist, and head down the hall toward my room. A guy I've seen around suddenly appears in front of me. He seems to have burst out of his dorm room.

"Hey, man," he says. "Was that you singing?"

"Yeah."

"You are really good."

"Thank you." I appreciate the compliment, but feel awkward as hell standing in my towel, dripping, trying not to drop my plastic soap dish and deodorant. I take a better look at the guy. Tall, reed thin, wild curly hair, a freshman. We've spoken a few times.

"Mark Bryan," he says. "I play guitar."

"Really?"

"Yeah." He absently strums his fingers on his door. He seems high energy, a man in motion. "You want to hang out later, have a couple of beers, see if we know any of the same songs?"

"Okay," I say.

I'm not sure why I agree to this. But something about this idea, this invitation, this kid. Plus, beer and music. Always music. I'm in, if only to hear this guy play, maybe join him in a song.

This eager, kind of intense kid—Mark—bows his head and knocks on his own door and says, "See you later, man."

"Darius," I say.

Later, I tape a note on my door for Carney, telling him to meet me down the hall at Mark's room. Mark has left the door open, so I walk in, swinging a six-pack. Mark sits at the edge of his desk chair, facing me, tuning his guitar. I don't know much about guitars, but I can tell a piece of junk from a serious instrument. Mark's guitar is professional grade. Then Mark starts to play and I feel myself smile. This kid can *play*. He starts strumming a song, looks up to see if I know it.

"R.E.M.," I say. "'So. Central Rain.'"

"You know R.E.M.?"

"*Love* R.E.M."

Mark goes into the song and when he gets to the chorus, I start singing, *"I'm sorry,"* and then we finish the song. We make eye contact and we sort of laugh, not talking about what we both just heard, what we both know—

That was pretty fucking good.

I start singing another R.E.M. song, "(Don't Go Back to) Rockville," and Mark immediately plays that. We sing yet another R.E.M. song and then "Take It Easy" by the Eagles, and then we do The Beatles, Simon & Garfunkel, The Police, Squeeze, both of us alternating the same question to each other before each song, "Hey, do you know . . . ?" and finding, incredibly, that we know all these songs, every word, every chord.

"Hey, man, how about this one?" I ask. "You know 'Family Tradition' by Hank Williams, Jr.?"

I start singing the first line of the song—*"Country music singers have always been a real close family . . ."*

Mark plays it perfectly, then stops abruptly.

"You don't know it?" I ask.

"No, I know it, I just—"

He laughs.

"What?"

"I didn't expect a Black dude would know all the words to a Hank Williams, Jr. song. Blows my mind."

"Oh, yeah? How about U2 and KISS? Love them. Now I'll seriously blow your mind. I *love* Barry Manilow."

"I must be really drunk. I thought you said Barry Manilow."

We crack up and then jump back into "Family Tradition,"

Mark singing the chorus and me harmonizing, belting *"Hank, why do you drink, Hank, why do you roll smoke."* We finish the song and hear applause. I turn and see Carney standing in the doorway, clapping, his spotlight of a smile streaming through the room.

"You got my note," I say.

"What note?"

"The note I left on my door."

"Didn't see it. I came down here because I heard music. You guys sound incredible."

And then, more applause. I look past Carney and see a group of kids from our floor clustered in the hall outside Mark's door.

"Free concert," someone says, and the group behind him cheers.

Mark and I keep going. I call out a song, Mark plays, I sing, we jam, more kids cram into the hall, more beer arrives, a lot more beer, hours pass, and Mark and I still keep going. Kids fill Mark's room and pack the hallway. Several pop open beers. A few knock back shots. Is this a concert or a party? Both. Whatever. We don't care. And then after one song as Mark tunes his guitar, I shout out, "Hey, Mark, let's do KISS. Do you know 'Rock and Roll All Nite'?" He answers by playing the intro. I jump in and sing, *"I wanna rock and roll all night, and party every day."*

. . .

Every night, for the next two weeks, I show up at Mark's room. He plays his guitar, I sing, the crowds gather in the hall, and the beer flows. As Mark plays and I sing a selection of our favorite songs, the crowd grows, singing along, clapping, drinking, dancing. Mark and I cover Springsteen; The Beatles; the Eagles; Hank Williams and Hank Williams, Jr.; Crosby, Stills, Nash & Young; Commodores; KISS; and R.E.M. Each night, a different jam, a concert, a party.

One afternoon, sitting around with Mark before our evening party, I blurt one word.

"Pappy's," I say.

Pappy's—beer, wings, big-screen TV, a student hangout—sits across the street from our dorm. Pappy, a crusty ex-marine, runs the place. We know Pappy is an ex-marine because he keeps the place stocked with marine paraphernalia, including his old helmet and jacket, and he has marine posters and photos plastered all over the walls.

"Let's ask him if we can play there."

Mark nods. "Branch out."

"Exactly. Instead of playing your room, let's go on the road."

"On the road. To Pappy's. Across the street."

"He'll love the idea."

Pappy doesn't love the idea.

Especially when I ask him to pay us fifty bucks to play Friday night.

"I'm not paying you fifty bucks. I never had a live band. I don't know if I *want* a live band. Why would I pay you anything?"

"We're not bad," I say.

"We're pretty good," Mark says.

"Yeah? Where have you played?"

"Around," I say. "We have a following."

Pappy stares at me.

"In our dorm," I say.

Pappy pauses and says, "I'll give you free beer if you don't suck."

I tell Carney and he takes care of the rest. He makes sure we'll be playing in front of a crowd and that the crowd will love us. In other words, he papers the house, making sure all our friends come and that they will drink.

A few minutes before we take the tiny stage at Pappy's, Mark and I realize that we need some sort of a plan, which later we'll learn is called a set list.

"What are we doing?" I ask Mark.

"What we do every night at the dorm."

"I know. I meant, what the hell are we *doing*?"

Mark laughs. "Don't worry about it. Take it easy."

And that's exactly how we start, with the Eagles' "Take It Easy." But before we begin, a friend of ours, Steve, whom we call the Wolf, jumps onto the stage in front of us.

"What are you doing up here?" I ask him.

"Introducing you," he says, and then, grabbing the mic, he shouts over the crowd that has packed the tables at Pappy's, "Hey everybody, how you doing?"

Everybody screams.

"Oh, *yeah!* You are in for a real treat tonight. Ladies and gentlemen, here are the very handsome and talented Mark Bryan and Darius Rucker—the Wolf Brothers!"

As the crowd applauds, and before Mark hits the first chord to "Take It Easy," I think, Nice, Wolf, you named us after yourself.

We finish "Take It Easy," then follow that up, not necessarily in this order, with "Feelin' Groovy," "Sail On," "Sultans of Swing," and after thirty minutes or so, we close with "Family Tradition."

The crowd at Pappy's goes insane. Kids stand the whole time, applauding constantly, and a few even join us onstage. The crowd is raucous and raunchy and drunk, really drunk, and I love it, every second of it. What's more, I want to do it again tomorrow, the next night, any night, every night.

After we finish our last song and we begin packing up Mark's guitar and small amp, Pappy approaches. I wouldn't call Pappy a warm, happy-go-lucky guy, but I'm pretty sure I see something resembling a smile curling across his face.

"That did not suck," he says. "Come back next week."

He starts to turn away, then comes back.

"I almost forgot."

He reaches into his pocket and hands me a fifty-dollar bill.

8

"SO. CENTRAL RAIN"

R.E.M.

We play three more gigs at Pappy's, packing the place each time, a line of kids forming outside the door, the party spilling into the street. I don't remember if Pappy pays us in cash or in beer after that first time. Maybe both. I have a vague memory of rolling a keg across the street to our dorm, into the elevator, and down the hall, but that may be a dream. I do remember that Mark and I—the Wolf Brothers—expand our repertoire of cover songs and extend the time we play from thirty to forty-five minutes and then to an hour. After that third time, I hear a difference. Mark and I are getting tighter. We improve with each performance. We don't just play, either. We practice, spending most evenings in Mark's dorm room working on our harmonizing, while I think about learning to play the guitar. Then Carney tells us that an organization of frat houses on campus wants to sponsor us to play at Russell House, the student union. No money, but exposure. Campus notoriety. The first time we'll be playing outside our dorm or Pappy's. This gig feels like a step up. This gig feels like a—*gig*.

We rock Russell House. I go home for Thanksgiving on a high, thinking only about music, listening to a new batch of songs that we might add to our set list, songs off the beaten path such as "I Go Wild" by The Three O'Clock and "In the City" by The Jam. I listen to these songs and I am struck by the thrumming bass, the pounding of the drums, the body-shaking fullness of the sound. When we return to campus, Mark and I arrive with the same thought. We want to expand. We want to go from a duo to a band.

We make the decision one night in his room. We agree to add a bass player and a drummer.

"You know that guy Dean Felber from upstairs, sixth floor?" Mark says. "We went to the same high school. We played in a band together. Fantastic bass player. I'll ask him."

He does.

Dean says no.

Mark asks again a few days later.

Dean says no.

"I'll ask him," I say one night.

I knock on Dean's door and a kid about my size, blue eyes, strong build, greets me. We know each other slightly and he invites me in. We start talking, pop open a couple of beers, I pull up a chair, and we talk and laugh and hang out. I can't put my finger on what is happening, but there is something so easy about us, a familiarity, like we've known each other before and we're picking up where we left off. Dean and I just *click*.

We talk school, sports, and, of course, music. Dean has a record on—*Abbey Road,* which we both consider The Beatles' seminal album. We spend an hour listening, not talking, then another hour listening, then we talk about the album, and music in general, occasionally shifting the subject to ourselves. Dean, a music savant, had gotten a music scholarship to Elon University, but turned it down to concentrate on business, finance, accounting, something in that world, maybe get an MBA. At least that's what he's told his parents. He's also told them, as he reveals during the third or fourth time through *Abbey Road,* that he promises he absolutely will not join a band. When I finally leave his room, I feel that Dean and I are not only friends, we could truly be best friends. It feels as if we've known each other for years.

I love this guy, I think. He's so laid-back it's painful. He reminds me of me.

"What did he say?" Mark asks me the next night. "Is he in?"

"I forgot to ask him."

The next night I do ask him.

Dean says no.

I ask him again—and again.

I ask him ten times, twelve times.

Each time he says no.

In the meantime, Dean and I have gone from really liking each other and becoming friends to becoming the closest of friends.

Finally, after the fifteenth or twentieth time I ask him to be our bass player, and the millionth time we've listened to *Abbey Road,* I say, "Come on, man, play with us. Just do it."

"I don't want to play with Mark again, man," he says. "He's too intense. He takes this shit so seriously."

"I'll handle that. Come on."

"Also—" He cracks open another beer. "I don't want to be in a cover band. I'm over playing covers. I want to play original songs."

"That's the plan. We're going to do new stuff."

"You're a cover band."

"For now," I say.

"Also—" Dean takes a swallow of his beer. "I promised my parents I wouldn't be in a band. Any band."

"Don't tell them."

He thinks about this. Takes his time.

"Hmm," he says finally.

"How they gonna know?"

"They'll know."

"Change your name."

"I don't think so."

"Okay, look, play with us once. We have a gig coming up. Play that gig. Then we'll find somebody else."

Dean looks dubious. "One gig?"

"One gig. That's it. Come on. You in?"

Dean sighs. "I'll do it. But only this one gig."

"Good. Now we need a drummer."

"Mark may know a guy. Phenomenal drummer."

"Awesome."

I spring to my feet, wobble a little, the beer causing my head to spin and sloshing in my gut. I start to head out the door. "We got a practice coming up. Mark's room. I'll let you know when."

"Only one gig," Dean says. "Until you find your bass player."

. . .

Mark does know a drummer—his former roommate's buddy Brantley Smith. Brantley also plays piano and cello and can sing his ass off. But when we invite him to join our band, he hesitates.

"I'm really busy with studying, playing cello in the university symphony and the string ensemble, and, you know, church."

Brantley, it turns out, is seriously Baptist. His parents definitely do not want him playing in a rock and roll band. But Brantley, being away from home, maybe feeling rebellious, agrees to join our band.

We decide to have our first rehearsal in his room, which is in a different dorm.

"Why do we have to go there?" Dean asks.

"Because it's easier for you and Mark to bring your amps to his dorm than for him to lug his whole drum set over here."

"Fair," Dean says. "Is he providing the beer?"

"He doesn't drink," I say.

"Shit," Dean says, considering this.

"I know," I say.

"Does he get high?"

"He's sober," I say. "Very religious, too."

After a moment, Dean says, "I don't care. I'm only doing this one gig."

. . .

Very early on, Dean and I fully embrace our shared passions—music, sports, and video games. And the familiarity I felt when I first hung out with Dean—that special, unnameable feeling—I can now identify.

Fraternity.

We are brothers.

Simply that.

We are inseparable, yes, but it's more than that. We share a sort of oneness. We do everything together, as in we spend *all* our time together. I can't imagine not being with him. I don't have to imagine it, actually, because we are virtually never apart. And when we're together, we don't even have to speak. We let the silence flow over us, locking us in. We are comfortable in silence. We can just *be*—not doing anything, not speaking, practically sharing the same breath. We are that close.

I have grown up with a close circle of friends. I know what that is. I know how that feels. This is different. Dean and I are two halves of a whole.

He is the brother I have always wanted.

. . .

Brantley, the drummer, is better than advertised. He's a musical prodigy, playing the drums like Stuart Copeland of The Police, blisteringly fast, punishing the drums, his hands a blur. Then he brings out his cello for "Eleanor Rigby," and harmonizes with me on several R.E.M. songs. We practice diligently but all of us itch to play in front of people, even Dean, who no longer mentions that he's agreed to play only one gig.

As before, our rehearsals become parties—kids congregating in the hall, swilling beer, knocking back shots, dancing, singing along, applauding, laughing, screaming, having a blast. Every so often, I glance at Brantley, to see how all this debauchery is going

down. He keeps himself an emotional distance away. He doesn't
partake in anything more than a soda. Plus, he's so into the music
that I don't think he really cares.

. . .

We need a name.

We have booked a gig beyond Pappy's. More than one, actually. We've been invited to play at a couple of frat houses and one
or two off-campus bars. We will get some kind of billing, on a
sign or something, and someone will introduce us.

But what will they say?

We don't have a name.

"Let's hear it for the Wolf Brothers and Two Other Guys"
won't cut it.

We need a *name*.

At rehearsals, we throw around ideas, all of them terrible. Because I'm Black and all the other guys have blue eyes, somebody
says, "How about Black and Blue?"

"Fuck *no*," I say.

And that's the best idea.

A few days before our first gig, our show choir, Carolina Alive,
performs a holiday concert at Myrtle Beach. We stay overnight at
a hotel and after the show a bunch of us convene in someone's hotel room for a game of quarters. Everyone in the group knows we
need a name for the band and between chugging drinks and trying
to flip quarters into a glass, people pitch names.

They got nothing.

Then—again—destiny.

Two guys in the show choir—Ervin and Donald, best friends—
walk into the hotel room together. Ervin has big round eyes and
wears thick glasses. He reminds me of an owl. I've begun calling
him Hootie the Owl and the name has caught on. His buddy,

Donald, has huge, bulging cheeks. He looks like the jazz trum-
peter Dizzy Gillespie.

"Hey, look," I say as Ervin and Donald walk in, "it's Hootie
and the Blowfish."

Time doesn't stop when I say that.

The people in the hotel room don't go silent and whisper, *That's it.*

But something happens.

I kind of know—right then—that Hootie & The Blowfish is *it.*

Our name.

It's not that the name is so great.

Well, it is sort of great.

The name is fun, light, tongue-in-cheek.

I say it aloud and the people sitting next to me say they like it.
Hootie & The Blowfish.

They really like it. *I'm* starting to like it.

The next night at band rehearsal, I pitch the name to the guys.

I think they'll hate it. But they're not sure. Sort of noncommittal. They throw out some other names. They all suck.

Finally, Mark says, "We're wasting time on this. We have to
rehearse. Let's keep the name for now. We can change it later."

Of course, once you name a band, it's hard to change it. So, we
don't. We keep the name. We call it our temporary name, a place-
holder, but the truth is, we *are* Hootie & The Blowfish. Period.

You might love the name or hate it.

But you won't forget it.

We start playing more gigs— frat houses, bars, restaurants that
are more upscale than Pappy's. We are now a full-throttle electric
bar band, unplugging only for a couple of songs. At first, we find
our groove and comfort zone with R.E.M. covers. At one gig, we
play thirteen consecutive R.E.M. songs. I count them. We probably play half of the songs on all their albums—*Murmur, Reckoning,
Fables of the Reconstruction.* To shake things up, we pop in a Beatles'
song, usually Brantley singing "Blackbird," then I'll do "In the

City" by The Jam or "I Go Wild" by The Three O'Clock. We talk about writing original songs but we're drawing crowds and the crowds want to hear covers. *Don't get off a winning horse,* I tell myself. And so far, Dean hasn't brought up leaving, even though we've gone well past that first gig.

We start booking regular gigs, three, four a week, still at frat houses, parties, bars, and other local music venues. And we're not only drawing larger and larger crowds, we're gaining a reputation.

Something different about them, I hear. *They're tight, they're fun, they play for hours. They have a unique sound—Black lead singer, three white dudes, great musicians, memorable name.*

In a matter of months, we become a successful local rock and roll band. And being a successful rock band means exactly what you think it means, and what Dean and I hoped it would mean—getting paid decent money and having easy access to a shit ton of booze and drugs. Oh, and sex. Women love rock musicians. Who knew? Well, everybody. During one afterparty involving excessive debauchery, even for us, I'm tempted to shout to Dean, *By the way, I found a bass player to replace you!*

Yeah. I don't see him quitting the band just yet.

. . .

Racism.

We're in South Carolina and you can't hide from it.

I don't ignore it. I try to steel myself against it. I don't know what else to do. I'm a singer in a rock and roll band. I just want to do my thing. Still, I'm human and when I hear someone say the N-word to me at a frat party, I want to stop the band from playing and fucking fight. I'm thankful that I often get buzzed before we go on because that takes the edge off my anger when something like that happens.

One time, after we set up to play at a frat party, I hit the head.

As Dean stands onstage, tuning up his bass, some drunken asshole yells a racist slur about me. Dean freezes. Glares at the guy. Then he packs up his bass and leaves.

I come back from the head and notice that Dean is gone.

"Where's Dean?"

The rest of the guys, who hadn't heard the frat guy's racist remark, look confused. Nobody saw Dean leave. Sometimes he does wander off.

We go in search of him. We search the rooms in the frat house. We go outside, check the house's grounds. Then I get the idea that Dean may have actually *left*.

I retrace our steps leading back to our dorm. I find Dean walking, halfway there. I break into a jog, catch up to him.

"Hey, man," I say. "What are you doing?"

"I'm not playing. Not at that house."

"What?"

He shrugs and keeps walking.

"Dean, what happened?"

He shrugs again, stops, toes the ground, and tells me what the asshole at the frat house said.

We both stand stock-still as if our feet are stuck in cement.

"Well, shit," I say.

"Yeah," Dean says.

"We could both leave. Fuck that guy. Fuck this gig."

"Yeah," Dean says.

"Or."

I pause.

"We could say fuck you by playing the shit out of this gig. We've got our band. He has fuck all."

"Racist dick," Dean says.

"Yes," I say.

Dean waits, thinks, then he nods.

"I'll play," he says.

We do play the shit out of that gig. We play for three hours. The crowd goes so crazy that they want us to play longer. As for Dean, I figure if he hadn't left tonight, he's never leaving. But he does tend to disappear, sometimes for no reason at all. It's at that moment that we make it official: Dean and I decide to room together. It's really a necessity to keep him from wandering off. So, my current job description: college student, lead singer in a rock band, and official bass player wrangler.

. . .

We branch out, start playing clubs in other towns, even in other states, performing up and down the East Coast. One highlight—we play a famous rock venue in D.C., The Bayou, which is on K Street in Georgetown. Dean, who's from Maryland, grew up seeing bands at The Bayou. And when I was about twenty, I went to The Bayou to see the Ramones, which is, to this day, the best show I have ever seen. Playing The Bayou—getting *paid* to play The Bayou—feels surreal to me.

We not only play The Bayou, we blow the doors off. A few weeks later, the folks at The Bayou book us again to perform on the same bill with some other bands during a big D.C. college weekend. To my shock, Dean invites his parents to see us play.

"Wait," I say. "I thought they were sort of opposed to you being in a rock band."

"Not sort of. Totally against it. They think I'm wasting my life. They want me to be an accountant."

I'm stumped. "Okay, so why—?"

Dean shrugs. "My parents like music. Maybe they'll see what we're about and, you know—"

"Change their minds?"

Dean shrugs again.

. . .

We meet Dean's parents in D.C. They take us to dinner before the show. Beautiful people, good food, good time. Dean and I pile into the back seat of their car and Dean's dad drives us to the gig. As we approach The Bayou, we see a line of people waiting to get inside. The line extends down the entire block, then keeps going, stretching down another block, then snakes down a *third* block.

"Who are all these people lined up to see?" Dean's dad says.

Dean hesitates. "I think they're waiting to see us."

Dean's dad makes a sound that falls somewhere between a clearing of his throat and a small laugh.

He thinks Dean is joking.

Nobody speaks while Dean's dad backs into a parking space several blocks away. We follow Dean's parents into The Bayou, passing the three-block-long line of people waiting to get in.

"They're never getting in," Dean's dad says.

The lobby is so clogged with people that we can barely squeeze inside. We inch our way to the ticket window to pick up Dean's parents' tickets, comped by Dean.

"You believe this?" the guy selling the tickets says. "You guys really draw. You're hot."

Dean's dad's jaw drops. He looks at Dean, takes a second, and then says, "They *are* here to see you."

"I guess we're starting to get noticed," Dean says.

The doors to the theater open then and the people who are jammed inside the lobby push forward, surging inside to grab seats. Dean's dad peers at the line of people outside, waiting, hoping to score tickets to our show.

"The line is three blocks long," he says, and repeats, softly, "They'll never get in."

He turns back and takes in Dean. His son. Future accountant. Until this moment.

He nods, then shares a look with Dean's mom. She nods back at her husband. They've decided. They've agreed.

Dean's dad rests his hand on Dean's shoulder.

"Alright," Dean's dad says. "You can do this."

A few months later, we play an outdoor amphitheater at a college in West Virginia. We perform before a thousand screaming, dancing, partying people, our wildest show yet.

After the show, Brantley quits the band.

His decision is not about the music. It's about us, his three bandmates and our lifestyle. More specifically, it's about our liberal involvement with drugs, alcohol, and women. We party. We party hard. We party hard before and especially after performances. For months, Brantley has observed this behavior from the sidelines with a quiet stoicism. An aloofness. Of course, he never partakes. Not once. Yet I have never felt or heard one word of disapproval or judgment. I sense only that he feels he doesn't belong. It's not only that our lifestyle isn't his scene. It's not his *life.* His belief system. The more popular the band becomes, the more we party, and the more Brantley embraces his sobriety and faith and the more he makes a conscious effort to separate himself. I see it, I feel it, and as time passes, I anticipate that he may be close to leaving the band. He just doesn't fit. The West Virginia gig becomes an inflection point. We reach new heights musically and sink to unprecedented depths of debauchery.

Afterward, as we all look at the gigs we have coming up, gigs that will bring us on the road more frequently, playing larger venues in bigger cities, promising a level of partying not for the faint of heart, Brantley tells us that he has come to a decision. He doesn't want to go on the road anymore. He realizes he has to give up the band. He tells us this quietly, sadly.

"I love playing with you guys and I love that the band is on the verge of something big, maybe something really big, but—"

He takes a second to collect himself.

"I can't do it. It's not who I am. Not who I want to be. I'm really sorry."

We understand. We really do. I know how hard it has been for him on the road. I tell him that I wish him well. I consider Brantley a friend, a good and honorable human being, a gifted musician and terrific singer. I respect his decision. He tells me how hard it was to make it. He prayed constantly, asking God to tell him what he should do. It took weeks, maybe months, but finally he emerged from a place of confusion and came to a realization. He believes that God did help him, did provide him the answer—to leave the band and take a different path with his life. I respect his process, his beliefs. Brantley stays true to himself. I admire that most of all. After Brantley leaves the band, he follows his faith, makes faith-based music, and becomes a minister.

9

"SHE TALKS TO ANGELS"

The Black Crowes

We schedule auditions for drummers at my house, eight in one day. Mark, Dean, and I now live off campus. I make a life choice: I decide to leave college the summer after my junior year. I want to devote all my time to the band. Plus, I'm drowning in debt from student loans. I don't see the point in finishing my degree and accumulating another year of staggering debt when I see a clear career path. Music. The band. I want to pay off my current loans and just play music. To earn some pocket money and keep myself busy during the day, I take a job at Sounds Familiar, a great local record store.

We begin the auditions. The drummers can all play, but they don't quite fit—with our sound, with us, with our dreams, with our drive. We've also changed our band's purpose, our definition. We're no longer just a cover band. We've begun writing songs. We don't collaborate. We write separately, in my case, when the mood hits. Mark and I write a couple of forgettable songs that we include in our set, one called "Calendar Girl," same title as the Neil Sedaka song. The resemblance ends there. Our early tries are basically R.E.M. knockoffs, mostly bad, but every now and then somebody brings in something that's a cut above, even eliciting an involuntary "wow" from one of us. Some songs show actual promise, even approach a level of pretty good. They do not suck. It's just that they don't quite—well, they do kind of suck. But we see the future—making our own music.

We begin the auditions for drummers. After jamming with the first five, I start feeling antsy. We've got gigs coming up and I'm constantly feeling a financial crunch. I want to get the band up and running again. I want to hit the road. We need a damn drummer.

Mark tells us about the next drummer coming in, number six. He's older, took a gap year, then came to the University of South Carolina as a soccer player. Super athlete and high-speed drummer who has played in a couple of local bands. Loves classic rock, enjoys playing covers, and he writes original songs.

"Guy's really wired," Mark says. "Hyperkinetic guy. Great drummer."

"What's his name?"

Mark looks at the list in front of him.

"Jim Sonefeld."

"*Soni* Sonefeld?"

"Yeah, that's him."

"No," I say. "Not happening. That fucker is not going to be in the band. No way. Fucking guy. I veto him."

Soni.

Oh, yeah, I know Soni.

. . .

Freshman year.

Before Hootie.

I'm eighteen years old.

Hormones raging. My mind consumed by exactly two things. Music and sex. Well, music and trying to have sex.

I'm singing in the Carolina Alive show choir and I meet Deb, a girl in the group, and I fall hard.

Deb and I start going out. I really dig her. But she only sort of digs me. The relationship—if you can call it that—feels very one-sided. I like hanging out with her and I know she likes hanging out with me, but that's about it. I'm hoping our hanging out leads to something more. I live in hope. I sometimes—hopefully—refer to Deb as my girlfriend.

One day, Deb calls me. She seems very excited, almost flustered. She invites me over to her dorm right then to hang out. She sounds insistent.

This is it, I think. I've broken through. Worn her down. Won her over. It—meaning some semblance of sex—is finally gonna happen.

I shower, get dressed, slap on cologne, and burn over to her dorm, which is all the way on the other side of campus. I arrive, breathless but acting as cool as can be, even though my heart is pounding in anticipation.

Very suavely, I start to close the door behind me. "So, you want to hang out, listen to some music, or, maybe—"

"Let's go to the sand volleyball courts," she says.

"The what?"

Deb takes my hand, entwines our fingers. "Come on. I want you to take a picture of me."

"Okay," I say. "Sure. But—"

But nothing. She leads me out of her room.

It's unbelievable what a guy will do for even the tiniest, slimmest *possibility* of sex.

We arrive at the sand volleyball courts and I get ready to snap a few photos so we can get the hell out of here and go back to her room.

"No, go to the top of the stairs," Deb says.

She has obviously thought this out.

"I want you to shoot the picture from up there, down at me, while I pose here."

"Great," I say. "Sounds very artistic."

I climb to the top of the stairs, look down to take the picture, and I see that Deb is posing next to something she has written in the sand.

I LOVE SONI.

Are you fucking kidding me?

I shout that—in my head.

I'm too stunned to speak. I consider Deb my girlfriend. She considers me her photographer. What a waste of time. Who the fuck is this Soni guy? I hate him.

Three years later, Mark studies my face. "So, wait. Soni stole your supposed girlfriend? Is that what this is about?"

"Yes. I was devastated. So fuck him."

"Did you take the picture?"

"Yes. I'm an idiot. I took the picture. Then she dumped me for him. I'm not allowing this fucker in the band."

Mark takes a deep breath. I think I catch him counting to three. "Fine. But just jam with him."

"Is he good?"

"He's very good."

"I'll jam with him. But that's it."

. . .

I may be a little cool, slightly standoffish toward Soni when we first start jamming. But once he starts playing, I forget about him and Deb. He's not only the drummer we all want and need, he's our missing piece. He arrives with our same shared sense of purpose. Call it, in my case, a maniacal drive. I want Hootie & The Blowfish to play more gigs, bigger arenas. I want us to explode. At one point, between songs, as we describe our plans for the band, Soni says, "Dream big. That's what I want, too. Shoot for the moon."

Shoot for the moon.

Exactly how I feel.

We jam some more, we talk some more, and I know that Soni is perfect for us. To close the door on the subject forever, I casually mention Deb and how he may have, unthinkingly, callously, stolen her from me.

"Who?" he says.

"She wrote your name in the sand at the volleyball courts."

"Oh, wait, yeah, I remember her. We hung out a couple of times. Nothing happened. Sometimes I get awkward around girls. I don't read the signs."

"She wrote your fucking name in the sand," I say. "Hard to miss that sign."

"Okay," Mark says, pointing his guitar at Soni. "We'll give you a call."

"Oh, one more thing," Soni says, reaching into his pocket and pulling out a cassette tape. "Mark told me you're starting to do originals. I wrote this song."

My memory of the next few moments has faded over time. I remember someone producing a cassette recorder. I remember the click as Soni presses "Play." I remember an acoustic guitar strumming a soft yet urgent instrumental introduction. I remember the first line of the song and how the lyrics grabbed me by the throat—

With a little love and some tenderness.

Then, a chord change, and I *feel* the next line. I actually shiver.

'Cause I wanna run with you.

I want to run with these guys, with this band.

That includes the new guy, this fucking Soni. Yeah, I want to run with Soni. Our drummer.

The song finishes, and Soni clicks off the cassette recorder.

"It's called 'Hold My Hand,'" Soni says.

For a moment, nobody speaks, and then I say, "I think we can cancel the other auditions."

. . .

Early 1990.

Mid–February or March, a Thursday or Friday night. The nights all blur, the weekends dissolve into a pulsing, shimmering haze, especially when the band isn't playing. These weekends, feeling antsy and bored, I tend to lose myself in drinking and heavy partying.

This night, I find myself at Monterrey Jack's, one of our local haunts. I sit at the bar hunched over a beer and a quesadilla as I bullshit with the bartender—Carney. I really can't afford to drink and eat here, but our friends own Monterrey Jack's and when money is tight, I eat and drink here for half price. These days, the cash flows out a lot more than it comes in. Or as the Simply Red song goes that Carney has playing over the sound system, *Money's too tight to mention.*

I polish off my beer and Carney snaps open another and plunks it down on the bar in front of me. I always take the same seat at the bar, first base as you walk in, my head right below the speaker. Carney plays DJ, popping in his favorite CDs all night long. Tonight I sit half listening to the music as Carney and I make plans for later, when his shift ends. We'll pick up Dean, then barhop, hit a couple of frat parties, and try to hook up with a trio of willing women. Your average Thursday night. Or is it Friday?

Carney slides out the Simply Red CD and puts on a new album called *Shake Your Money Maker* by a band out of Atlanta, the Black Crowes. Three guys, led by two brothers, Chris and Rich Robinson. Their hit single, "Hard to Handle," is all over the radio. I like the song, but not enough to buy the album yet, even with my employee's discount at Sounds Familiar. I hoover my half-price quesadilla, debate whether I have the stones to ask Carney for another, decide I don't, then peer into my beer glass, swirl the beer, and sit staring at the golden liquid. I lift my head and study the walls, trying to avoid wallowing any further in my cash flow problem.

Carney moves to a couple of newly arrived customers. I drum my fingers on the bar and listen to the Black Crowes album. Carney returns and we bullshit some more, he washes and dries some shot glasses, moves to serve some cocktails, and a song comes on, blasting through the speaker, right above my head.

The opening guitar riff freezes me.

The music—catchy, acoustic—shakes me.

Uh oh. I'm starting to get that feeling.

Then it happens. Chris Robinson sings the first line of "She Talks to Angels"—

She never mentions the word "addiction"—

And I'm gone.

I feel myself turning toward the music—I'm ten inches away from the speaker—and I still don't feel I'm close enough. I want to get inside the music. I want to get inside that song. And then, somehow, I do. I'm pulled in. I lose myself in the urgency of Chris's voice. I am no longer at Monterrey Jack's. I have drifted away. I'm yanked into space. Only when the song ends, five and a half minutes later, do I return to earth, plunk, sitting back on my barstool.

Another song from the album comes on, then another. I don't really hear them. Carney drifts by again. He must see something in my face, a dazed look in my eyes, or my mouth wide open, gaping, because he says, "Hey, what's up?" He may even snap his fingers in front of me.

"Carney, you got to play that song again."

"What song?"

"That Black Crowes song."

"I just played it."

"Dude, please, *please*—play it again."

"Alright, alright."

He pulls out the CD, finds "She Talks to Angels" on the album, and plays the song again.

I close my eyes this time and when the song ends, I say aloud, "You got to be kidding me. Holy shit. Holy fucking *shit*."

"You okay? You need some water?" Carney says.

"Play the song again, please."

He doesn't want to and I understand. Paying customers drinking at a bar don't love hearing the same song over and over, but Carney slips it into the rotation two or three times over the next hour. But it's not enough. Not nearly enough.

"I got to go," I say. "I'll catch up with you later."

I speed walk to another bar a few blocks away. I know the bartender, as in I've hooked up with her a couple of times. She waves as I walk in. I go right up to her and I say, "You know the Black Crowes? You've got to play 'She Talks to Angels.' Please. It's the third to last song on the new album."

She puts on the song. I order a beer. The song ends. I finish the beer, order another, and my bartender friend plays the song again. I drink another beer and the bartender plays the song *again*.

"That song," I say, slapping a big tip onto the bar, fuck my cash flow, "that fucking *song.*"

I stagger out of the bar and head next door to Group Therapy, another bar we frequent, my favorite hangout, and I go straight up to George, the bartender, and my words slurring, I say, too loudly, nearly shouting, "George, the Black Crowes. Please play this 'She Talks to Angels' song. Please. *Please.*"

He plays it. And plays it. I drink another beer, or two, I've lost count, and George plays "She Talks to Angels" again, and by this time, I know all the words. But I don't sing along. I won't. I can't. I have to listen. I have to take this song in. Absorb it. Live it. Allow the song to enter my skull, creep into my DNA, seep into my soul. Oh, man, I am drunk, shit-faced, blotto, but this song, this fucking *song.* I tip George twenty, my last twenty, and somehow I stumble my way home. I try to shake the song off. I need to listen to something else, but not just anything, something great, so I put on an older Bonnie Raitt CD, *Home Plate,* crank up the volume so loud the floorboards buckle, and then I power up the PlayStation and start playing *Madden.* Bonnie growls through "What Do You Want the Boy to Do?" and then I'm howling the song "Good

Enough" along with her, crying, *"First time I brought you home, my mama said he ain't good enoughhh . . ."* I sing every song on the album with her, all the way to the last one, joining her in a country singalong of "Your Sweet and Shiny Eyes."

The album ends, the game ends, my mouth feels dry, my head swims, the room sways. I look down, and I'm holding my guitar—how did it get there? I don't remember—and I look at the strings, all of them blurring into one long taut silver river, and I say, "I am going to write my own 'She Talks to Angels' song and someday I'm going to give it to Bonnie Raitt."

I strum a chord, and I start singing a melody, and a song pours out of me, like some sort of miracle, the words flowing out of my head, out of my mouth, tumbling over each other, everything happening in a stream of consciousness, and I lean over and hit "Record" on the little four-track next to me, and I go back to the beginning of this song, my song, and I sing it straight through. I play it back, and I then I sing the whole song again, changing a phrase here, a line there, a lick here, hit "Record" again, and I sing it one more time, putting down this second version, singing nonstop, going all the way through with these little changes. I turn off the four-track, and close my eyes.

The next thing I know it's tomorrow. I wake up, spread out in my bed. I'm pretty sure it's late afternoon, or maybe early evening. I see Dean walking by my open door, on his way to firing up *Madden.*

"Dude," I say.

My mouth feels like it's filled with sand. I can't speak. I force myself out of bed and join Dean in the living room. I swallow and try again to formulate words.

"Dude. Last night."

"Yeah?"

"I went way past drunk."

"I saw."

"I wrote a song."

"Yeah?"

"We should listen to it. I bet it's pretty funny."

"Let's definitely listen to it," Dean says. "I bet it's funny as hell."

I find the four-track, hit "Play," and the song I wrote comes on. It finishes and Dean stares at me.

"That's not funny."

"No," I say.

"Not funny at all. It's fucking *good*."

"I should play it again."

I do and this time when the song ends, I stare at Dean. "It *is* good."

We play it again and this time we both crack up when my slightly cracked voice sings, *She says, 'Dad's the one I love the most, but Stipe's not far behind.'*

Love and honor R.E.M.

"We got to put this song into the set," Dean says.

The band learns the song and we introduce it two weeks later at the Georgia Theatre in Athens. After the show, as we pack up our gear, a guy approaches the stage. He weaves a little as he walks. He's clearly high on something and quite happy.

"Hey, man," he says, waving his hand at us. "What's the name of that new song y'all played tonight? It's great."

I look at Mark. He shrugs.

"Glad you like it," I say. "We haven't named it yet. It's brand-new. We just wrote it the other day."

The guy scrunches his forehead and nods. "Well, man, hell, if she's going to cry, fuck her, let her cry."

Mark and I look at each other and I say, "Yeah."

I turn back to the guy. "Thanks, man."

"For what?"

"The title. The song's called 'Let Her Cry.'"

10

"I WISH IT WOULD RAIN"

Nanci Griffith

I can't go there.
My skin's the wrong color.

<small>FROM "I DON'T UNDERSTAND," HOOTIE & THE BLOWFISH</small>

I can feel it.

We're on the verge.

The verge of . . .

Popularity. Recognition. And taking the next steps with the band, creatively.

We've essentially done away with covers now and have focused on originals. I have caught the writing bug. I write constantly. I know I'll never repeat that stream-of-consciousness experience that led to "Let Her Cry." But now, when I write, I go deeper. I get reflective and I get personal. I start putting myself, my perspective, my emotions, and even my politics into songs.

And I put in my hurt. Meaning—racism. I write "I Don't Understand," a song that talks about how I can't go to certain places because of the color of my skin, and I write "Drowning," a purely political song dealing with race.

I really let loose in "Drowning."

I write—

Why is there a rebel flag hanging from the statehouse walls?

I also ask the following question because I really want to know.

Just 'cause you don't look like me, tell me, what do you see?

I close the song this way.

Oh, drowning, hating everybody else 'cause they don't look like you.

The band supports these songs because they not only support me, they have seen and heard racism firsthand before and after shows. We're a Southern band, after all, and racism runs rampant in the South and the racist divide cuts deep. More than once, after hearing some faceless fool hiding in the crowd in front of us shouting the N-word, the guys, usually led by Dean, start packing up their instruments and get ready to leave. More than once, Dean does leave.

"Welcome to my world," I say to the guys. I never ignore what I hear, I never excuse it, I never accept it. But if I allow the racism to stop me—to stop us—then racism wins. I deal with it by hardening myself. I develop rhinoceros skin.

Hating me because I don't look like you.

I hear it, I hear you, I get it, you hate me.

But you can't beat me.

. . .

One time, while composing a song, I get some help from my mom.

I have the chorus down, *I only wanna be with you,* and I've added a reference to the greatest lyric writer of all time, Bob Dylan.

Put on a little Dylan . . .

Ain't Bobby so cool

I only wanna be with you

Yeah I'm tangled up and blue.

The song's not finished, I know that. The song needs something more, something personal. I toy with a few ideas. Nothing feels or sounds right. I feel stuck.

One Sunday afternoon, I take a break from songwriting to watch my beloved Miami Dolphins play the New York Jets. As the Dolphins blow a lead and fall behind, well on their way to another unbearable loss, my mom calls. One thing you have to understand. I am not a Dolphins fan. I am a Dolphins fanatic. I bleed Dolphins aqua. I live and die on every pass, run, punt, and defensive possession. I immerse myself in every Dolphins game, watching with a deep, passionate, emotional attachment that borders on the unhealthy.

So, when my mom calls, I have only moments ago witnessed and endured yet another painful Dolphins collapse. The team has broken down and I am breaking down. I shouldn't even answer the phone when it rings, but I do. I barely burble a hello.

"Darius? Is that you?"

"Oh, yeah, hi, Mom."

"What are you doing?"

"Nothing. Watching TV."

"You don't sound right. What's wrong?"

I sniff, try to fight back tears, fail.

"Wait," my mom says. "Are you watching the Dolphins game? Are you—crying?"

"No, no, fighting a cold."

"You are crying. You're watching the Dolphins and you're crying."

"No, no, I'm not, I—"

"Unbelievable. The Miami Dolphins are making you cry again."

"It's just that I—"

"Damn, boy, that is pathetic. Call me back when you grow up."

She hangs up and I have to agree—my obsession with the Miami Dolphins is sort of pathetic and childish. I can't help it. It's real. And it's who I am. But soon after my mom's phone call, something clicks. A lyric comes to me. I finish that stalled song with these lines.

Sometimes you're crazy and you wonder why
I'm such a baby, yeah, the Dolphins make me cry . . .
I only wanna be with you.
Thanks, Mom.

. . .

Around this time, we add a new member to our team—Chris Carney. At the beginning, Carney was always around. He came to our first band practice, the first show, and every show after. He hauled equipment, organized cars to drive us, including driving his car, and of course partying with us. But after he finished college, as the band hit the road, Carney went his own way. He got married and became a police officer. Perfect. A professional protector. He does well—Carney always does well—but after being on the force for three years, he asks to meet me one night for drinks. I've been on the road with the band and Carney and I haven't seen each other much. We catch up, we talk, we laugh, our connection feeling as strong as ever. At one point, he takes a sip of his drink, and goes quiet.

"I want to talk to you," he says. "If there's any way you might have a job for me, I'd like to interview for it."

"You're a police officer," I say. "We can't pay you what you're making."

"Darius," Carney says. "I make twenty-one thousand dollars a year."

"Shit, I'll pay you that just to hang out with me."

He pounds back his drink. "I'm giving my two-weeks notice tomorrow."

On his next-to-last day as a police officer, Carney signs off his shift and goes home. He greets his wife and his baby daughter, Hannah Jane. Suddenly, he hears screaming. He runs outside and sees his neighbor, a single mom, in her front yard. Her ex-boyfriend stands next to her. He holds a gun to her head.

I've been a cop for three years and I've never drawn my gun, Carney thinks. Here I am, my last night, and this happens.

Carney races back inside his house, instructs his wife to take their daughter into the bathroom and lock the door. He calls 911, grabs his shotgun, charges back outside, and locks his front door.

Carney crouches behind his car and levels his shotgun at the man with the gun.

"I'm a police officer," Carney says. "Put the gun down."

The man doesn't move. He stares at Carney.

"Put the gun *down*," Carney says again, aiming the shotgun at the man's chest. "Please."

The man keeps his eyes locked on Carney. After a moment, he lowers the gun to his side. He moves away from his ex-girlfriend.

He starts walking slowly toward Carney.

A front yard away.

Fifty feet separates them.

The man keeps walking.

"Stop!" Carney shouts. "Put the gun down! *Stop!*"

The man keeps walking.

Forty feet away.

Thirty feet.

Carney's face pulses red. His voice croaks as he screams: "DROP THE GUN!"

His throat feels raw, on fire.

The man slowly, slowly walks toward him. He keeps walking.

Twenty feet away.

Five more steps, Carney thinks. If he takes five more steps—

He presses one eye closed as he looks over the barrel of the shotgun.

My daughter and my wife are inside. I have no choice. The second he steps onto my property, I am going to shoot him.

Carney eases his finger onto the trigger of the shotgun.

He aims at the center of the man's chest.

At first, he doesn't even hear the police cruisers screaming into his driveway and slamming to a stop in front of his house. But in his periphery, he sees a battalion of cops charging and tackling the man with the gun. Carney exhales, lowers his shotgun, and stands up behind his car. Only then does he realize that he is shaking. An officer approaches. "You alright?"

"I almost killed him," Carney says.

The officer nods and doesn't speak.

"One more day," Carney says.

Carney makes it through the next day—his final day as a police officer—and we hire him to oversee our outdoor events. Time ticks by. I write the song "Hannah Jane" about his daughter. The song becomes the first song on our first album, *cracked rear view*. Carney steadily moves his way up in our organization, and our lives, doing everything from arranging our gigs to hiring and firing crew, to overseeing every aspect of the band. He is our go-to guy when it comes to all things Hootie, becoming our eyes and ears, and then *my* eyes and ears, and then my business manager. Then and still. Carney pays the bills, buys the insurance, invests my funds, keeps the checkbook. He is the only person in the world who can tell me no—and he does, all the time. Simply, Carney is indispensable.

. . .

We all agree. The band needs a calling card, a demo cassette that we can give to record producers and managers in the hope that somebody will sign us and take us to that next level. Currently, we're producing and managing ourselves. We're doing fine, maybe better than fine, but to most people, we're a popular bar band with a funny name. I know we're much more.

After a gig at Greenstreet's, one of our favorite venues in Columbia, at around three in the morning, we convince the sound guy to record a demo cassette for us. We play five original songs, including "Hold My Hand," all in one blistering take each. Even though the sound quality is less than ideal, we make a bunch of copies, which we vow to hand out to anyone with clout, with connections—hell, to anyone who will listen.

A few weeks later, we play a dark and depressing club in Raleigh known for booking punk and heavy metal bands. We open for a local rockabilly band, neither of our bands really a perfect fit for the venue. We don't care, it's a paying gig, and we play our asses off in front of a fairly indifferent crowd, among them Dick Hodgin, the manager of the other band. Knowing he's in the audience stirs us up. Everyone knows about Dick Hodgin. He's one of the most influential record producers and managers in the South. After the gig, Mark finds him, appeals to him, and presses a copy of our demo cassette into Dick's polite but less than enthusiastic hands. He promises to listen, but he raises an eyebrow as he reads the name of our band on the label of the cassette. You can tell when someone isn't crazy about our name. I can also tell when someone—in this case, Dick—*hates* the name. As we head out of the club, I chalk this up as a waste of a tape. I know he'll never listen to the cassette.

I'm right. He doesn't listen to it. He hands the cassette off to his young assistant, Rusty Harmon. Not only does Rusty listen to it, he flips. He loves the music, our frenetic pace, our style, our songwriting. He implores his boss to listen to the band with the crazy name.

"You *have* to listen to this," he says.

Hodgin does. He makes his decision after listening to the first three songs—"I Don't Understand," "Little Girl," and "Look Away." He turns to Rusty and says, "I hear what you mean. I get it. Book a recording session." Rusty contacts Mark and only a couple of weeks after Dick Hodgin hears our primitive demo cassette, the four of us head to Raleigh for five days. In between touring the town, drinking, barhopping, and clubbing, we record our first demo tape in a professional studio, laying down five original songs—"I Don't Understand," "Little Girl," "Look Away," "Let My People Go," and "Hold My Hand." I sing with deep conviction, raw emotion, and the band absolutely rocks behind me. We play hard, we play fast. We want to sound like R.E.M. No. That's not right. We want to *be* R.E.M. After listening to the final edited cut of the demo tape, I lean back in my chair, and I murmur, low, "This fucking kicks *ass*." I still consider that demo cassette one of the best things we've ever recorded. Back then, I do know this much. We have created a real calling card, a strong introduction to the band.

. . .

We need professional help. Now that we have a serious demo tape, we have to hire a real manager, someone who can book gigs for us, keep us working, and at some point, lead us to a record deal. Dick likes us, sees promise in us, but he has so much on his plate that we can't imagine he would give us his full attention. We want to stay connected to him, though, so we ask Rusty, who's about to graduate college, if he'll bring us into Hodgin's company and serve as our manager-booker. He agrees.

The next year we work nonstop. Hitting the road in a ratty, beer-infused white Ford Econoline, it seems that we play every frat, club, and midsized venue in South Carolina, North Carolina, Virginia, and Maryland. We branch out sometimes, too, playing gigs in D.C. and as far north as Boston. In the spring, we play a festival in Florida where we perform in front of two thousand screaming fans. Word about the band with the crazy name spreads. We're fast, fun, and we deliver a set of smoking-hot original songs. People who attend our concerts call our shows a party. It's true.

And we party hard. Before we hit the stage, we down shots of Jägermeister. During our shows, we down shots of Jägermeister. After the show, a lot more Jägermeister. We play high, we play drunk, but we play. Maybe I'm too high to know, but the drink and drugs seem to enhance my singing. The drink and drugs also add to the party, and sometimes amp us up. Mark, who doesn't indulge anywhere close to the rest of us, really goes crazy. He struts on the stage, he windmills his guitar, he even strips, ripping off his shirt, and one time pulls down his pants and plays in his underwear. The crowds roar. They adore us, losing themselves in the experience of our shows, loving the music, our performance, everyone participating in the party.

We also expand musically. We add a bunch of new songs, many of them more complex musically and lyrically. Then almost exactly a year after we record our first five-song demo tape, Dick suggests that we put out a second demo cassette, one that reflects our musical growth. Again with Dick's guidance, we return to the studio and record a demo we call *Time,* four songs—"Running From an Angel," "Time," "Let Her Cry," and "Drowning." As we listen to the demo tape, I hear the difference from the first demo. I hear our growth. We've become both a tighter and a looser band. We've let go of that early, frenetic R.E.M.-like sound and become something else, still rocking and fun, but deeper, more reflective. We've definitely grown—into ourselves.

. . .

Late October, 1992.

We've been playing nonstop, three, four, five shows a week, packing every venue we play, drawing wall-to-wall crowds, usually standing room only because the bars and clubs we play don't have a lot of chairs. Then, one day, out of the blue, I get a call from my mom.

"I'm coming to see you," she says.

"Oh," I say, yawning, feeling groggy, slightly hungover. I also feel thrown off. My mother never comes to see me in Columbia. "When?"

"Tomorrow."

I sit up. "Tomorrow? Okay. Great."

"Don't worry," she says. "I'm only coming for the day. I'm not moving in or anything."

"That's good. Seriously, I want you to come. It's been too long. I want to see you."

"See you tomorrow," she says.

I hang up, feeling—I'm not sure what. Surprised, for sure. But also happy. We've been so busy playing clubs in Columbia and on the road that I haven't kept as closely in touch with my mom as I would like, as I should. It's been a while since we've spent time together. It's been literally years since we spent an entire day together, probably not since I was a kid. We're overdue to have a visit.

My mom comes up from Charleston, about two hours away. She arrives early so we can have the whole day. I plan everything. We start at the Riverbanks Zoo and Garden. We take our time, soaking up the crisp fall air, stopping to check out the zebras, the giraffes, the lions. Afterward, we wander through the lush botanical gardens, hang out in the warmth of the greenhouses. After the zoo and the botanical gardens, we head over to the statehouse and spend some time going through the South Carolina State Museum. After our full day of taking in the sights of Columbia, I take her on my personal Hootie & The Blowfish tour of Columbia, showing her the clubs and bars where we frequently play. My mom has never seen us play in person. This is more my choice than hers. I don't want her to stand for three hours in some cramped, smoky bar. As a nurse, she has spent a lifetime on her feet. I want her to sit down, relax, and hear us play. I want her to see us when we hit it big, playing in a coliseum or arena. That's my dream, my wish. I know it will happen. I can visualize us playing in front of a stadium audience, but so far, that's all it is, an imaginary performance.

"You will hit it big," she says. "I have no doubt."

After my personal Hootie tour, we go to dinner. I splurge and take her to the best restaurant in town.

We don't say much at dinner. We don't have to. We have the ability to enjoy being together, enjoying each other's company. We make small talk, we gossip, and we laugh, how we laugh. I feel as if I have been laughing with Mom all day. I've certainly had a smile on my face from the first second I saw her, walking into my living room. I'm just so happy to be spending time with her. I feel like a kid again, stealing special time with her, the two of us, the way we always would when I lived in Charleston.

After dinner, we go back to my place. I offer her a beer, and to my surprise, she accepts. I laugh at that, too. Yes, she's my mom, but I have to remind myself that she's also Carolyn, an adult who enjoys an adult beverage. Of course, I've seen her snap open her cans of Budweiser before, but not with me as her drinking buddy. But here we are, for the first time ever, two adults, sitting at my kitchen table, drinking, talking, laughing. It feels strange and—awesome.

For a few moments, we sit across from each other, silently sipping our beers. We've just shared a laugh about something and we're letting the residue of that giddy, warm feeling cloak us. I suddenly heave a sigh and look at my mom. Really look at her. We've never been a demonstrative family. We don't do much hugging or proclaiming about how much we love each other. We know it. We feel it. We just don't express it very much.

But this night, something comes over me, and I say, my voice cracking, "Mom, I want to thank you for putting up with me."

"What do you mean? I didn't put up with you."

"Well, you worked so hard, a single mom, working double shifts, sacrificing yourself to make ends meet for us. You went out of your way for all of us. You were always there for me. I want you to know how much I appreciate you."

"I know you do, Darius."

I smile. "I remember when I used to play Pop Warner. I wanted you to see me play. I knew how hard it was for you to make my games. You said you'd come but I'd be worried that you wouldn't be able to. I understood if you couldn't make it. But I'd look up and there you were, still wearing your work clothes, walking down the little path from the sidewalk to the field. I'd burst out smiling, so happy that you made it. You even came to the games when I didn't play quarterback. I'd be the tight end or the right tackle and you could barely pick me out on the field, but you were there."

My mom sniffs, dabs her eyes with her sleeve.

"You were a great mom," I say. "And you did everything yourself, with no help."

My mom lowers her head as the tears come.

"And now, I just want you to be proud of me," I say.

"Darius, I'm so proud of you."

"I want you to know that everything I do, I'm doing for you. I want to succeed for you. I'm going to make it. I swear I am. I'm going to take care of you because you took care of me. I'm going to be that son who buys you the biggest house you ever saw, the biggest house you ever dreamed of—"

We both lose it.

We stand at the same time, kick our chairs back, and we hug, clinging to each other, both of us sobbing, the tears gushing down our cheeks.

"I love you, Mom," I say.

She nods, and says, "I love you so much."

What a day, I think after she leaves. What a beautiful, unforgettable day.

· · ·

A week later, my aunt calls me on the phone.

My mother has had a heart attack.

She has lapsed into a coma. She is unresponsive.

I feel my hand shaking as I hold the phone.

"I'll be there tomorrow," I say.

"No," my aunt says.

"I'm coming."

"Darius, she's in a *coma*. She won't even know you're here."

I pause, frozen, unsure what to do. Should I wait, leave in a few days, or should I head up to Charleston immediately?

"Do you have any shows this week?" my aunt asks.

"I've got three shows."

"Play your shows. Your mom would want that. She would insist that you play your shows."

I lower my head to my chest.

I know my aunt is right. My mom would tell me to play the shows. She would tell me to go to work.

So I do.

I play the three shows and then I go to the hospital in Charleston. I walk into her room and see my mom in a stark, well-lit room, lying in a hospital bed. She is unconscious, immobile, her body attached to a tangle of wires and tubes. A machine at her side monitors her heart and her breathing, occasionally emitting a low, sharp beep. The room smells both sterile and fragrant from flowers in vases on her night table. I carry a chair over to her bedside. I reach for her hands, touch them gently, and stare at her frail body, barely a ripple beneath the bedsheet. Then, for some reason, a song comes into my head. I hesitate and then I begin singing Nanci Griffith's "I Wish It Would Rain."

Oh, I wish it would rain
And wash my face clean.
I want to find some dark cloud to hide in here
Love in a memory . . .

I sing the song all the way through, and then I pause for a moment, and I sing it again, fighting back sobs as I sing—

Oh, love in a memory sparkled like diamonds
When the diamonds fall, they burn like tears.

I finish the song and then I sing it *again*.

I hold for a beat after I finish, take a breath, and then I sing Nanci Griffith's song again—and again—and *again*—

I sing "I Wish It Would Rain" at least one hundred times.

I don't consciously choose this song. It just happens. I love Nanci Griffith's gorgeous melody and her moving lyrics, especially at this moment, sitting by my mother in her hospital bed. Lately, I've been listening to Nanci's album *Little Love Affairs* constantly and especially to this song, the eighth or ninth cut. Every song on the album has become my current jam, but I cannot get "I Wish It Would Rain" out of my head. The song grips me every time I hear it. But today, the song relaxes me, settles me, enables me to sit for hours, holding my mom's hands, hearing her soft breathing punctuated by the mesmerizing rhythm of the *beep-beep-beep* from the monitor. Singing the song soothes me and repeating it over and over, losing myself in the lyrics and the melody, I almost feel as if I'm praying.

I look at her in the hospital bed and I know that my mother will never hear our band play. She will never see me sing on a big stage. As hard as it is for me to admit, I know that she will never hear me sing again. I hold her hands a little bit tighter, drop my head, and mutter a prayer. I pray to God. I thank God for my mother. She has left this world—my world—a better place. I pray that if she does pass now that she will leave this world in peace and without pain.

I lift my head, dab my eyes, and sing "I Wish It Would Rain" again. And again. I keep on singing that song. I sing for her. I sing for this beautiful woman, this generous, loving, giving soul. My mother. And I believe as I sing that somehow she can hear me. I believe that with all my heart. This is her final concert, the concert that she is supposed to hear, a concert for the two of us, connecting the same way we did the day and night a week or so ago, connecting as we always have during my entire life with her, deeply, lovingly, with our whole hearts, our souls, not needing to speak, just feeling each other, *connecting,* through music, through a song.

. . .

After I spend the day by my mother's bedside, my aunt convinces me to go on the road for the rest of our scheduled gigs.

She would want you to go. That would be her wish.

I leave the hospital, my heart weighing a ton, but I truly believe that my mom would want me to go back to work. Twenty-four hours after I sing "I Wish It Would Rain" by her bedside—November 1, 1992—my aunt calls me. My mom has passed away.

"How old was she?" someone asks me later.

"Is," I say. "*Is.*"

I cannot speak of my mom in the past tense. I can't.

My mom is fifty-one years old.

I refuse to abandon the band. I play the two remaining shows that week, as scheduled, and then I go back to Charleston to attend my mother's funeral. I barely speak during the ceremony or afterward. But I said this then and I say it now.

Mom, I sing every song for you.

Every single song.

11

"DETROIT ROCK CITY"

KISS

From November 1992 and into the first few months of 1993, we play nonstop, gig after gig, earning around $55,000 each, more than what our friends are making, and not bad for a hard-charging bar band without a record deal. We play nearly fifty gigs in the first quarter of the year so we earn our pay. Meanwhile, all four of us work other jobs to support our playing-in-a-rock-and-roll-band habit. Mark moonlights as a videotape editor at Channel 57 in Columbia, Soni works at the University of South Carolina putting together instructional sports videos, and Dean, my man, tends bar. But as we rock toward summer, we start seeing a future in which we could conceivably give up our jobs and focus solely on our music. I consider leaving Sounds Familiar, my record store hangout and place of employment, but only for a nanosecond. I love working there, love hearing new music the moment it comes out, and I *love* getting discounts on albums. I'll stick it out at Sounds Familiar, at least for the time being.

Meanwhile, we continue to play and party hard. Crowds continue to have a blast at our shows. I live the lyrics from the KISS song "Detroit Rock City"—

Everybody's gonna move their feet
Get down

Everybody's gonna leave their seat . . .
Get down!
KISS. My current jam.

I can't get enough of these guys—Paul Stanley, Gene Simmons, Ace Frehley, and Peter Criss—their costumes, their makeup, their glam, their attitude, and their headbanging music. I blast their albums. Thankfully, Dean likes them as much as I do. Well, I think he does. At least he never complains, never asks me to lower the volume. But he wouldn't. He's too chill. Nothing fazes him. We've become even closer than we were before. We're basically two bodies with one brain. We're more than brothers. We're Siamese twins. If I like a band and listen to their album a million times in a row, Dean likes them just as much as I do. Or he indulges me. He understands why I go crazy over a particular artist or album and he goes along for the ride as well.

He digs KISS, but sees that it's much more than that for me. I *need* KISS. All the time. Maybe he figures that I'm going through a phase and that I'm trying to lose myself in this heavy metal music as an escape, especially from thinking about my mom. I don't know. I think I just like KISS. For sure, my mom is always on my mind, but I don't talk about my feelings very much. I internalize my pain, my sadness. I do write songs about her. I strum chords and scribble thoughts, emotions, memories. For a while, it seems that every song I write is about her. I write two songs in particular about my mom that explode from my heart, "I'm Goin' Home" and "Not Even the Trees." Both will appear on our first album, along with a "hidden track" that closes the album—"Motherless Child," a traditional, heartrending spiritual that expresses exactly how I feel. Sometimes I sing that song alone in my room. The whole song takes less than a minute, but I can barely get through it without crying.

Sometimes I feel like a motherless child . . .
A long, long way from my home
My soul aches when I sing that song.

And while I don't talk much about my mother's passing to anyone, not even Dean, the song "I'm Goin' Home" tears me up. I start with two lines that bring me right back to her bedside, in her hospital room.

Mama, please don't go
Won't you stay for one more day?

Sometimes, late at night, after a gig, lying in bed unable to sleep, I whisper those lines.

I remember that day my mom and I spent in Columbia.

That beautiful day. That special day.

How I wish we could've had one more day.

. . .

It's happening. We find ourselves in the center of buzz. Heat. After five years of playing bars and driving in our ratty van to gigs in East Nowhere, South Carolina, someone who's somebody momentarily anoints us the hot new thing. Men in suits appear and descend. Record company executives emerge. Managers negotiate. Lawyers draft contracts. And then we have a record deal. Only a matter of ironing out the details, plowing through and translating boilerplate legalese on contracts. Then the final, final, *final* step. All we have to do is get ourselves to L.A. on our own dime (will the ratty van make it?), sign the final, final, *final* documents, deposit our thirty or whatever thousand dollars—I never was good with knowing exactly how much money we're talking about, that's Carney's department—and record our first album.

Is this real? This can't be real.

Oh, it's real, Darius. A sure thing. The real deal.

Okay, if everybody says so, but let me get this straight—

We have to go to L.A. to sign the contracts? They don't have pens in South Carolina?

Suits nodding enthusiastically, lawyers speaking in paragraphs, or as I call it, billable hours, and then somehow, I buy into the hype, rise above my usual healthy skepticism, and give in. I allow myself to feel the excitement the other guys feel. It's really happening. *A record deal. We are going to L.A. and we're going to cut our first album.* I am STOKED!

Then, of course, everything falls apart. Collapses. Turns to shit. I'm initially deeply disappointed, make that crushed, but I shake it off. It all seemed too good to be true, and as my mom always said, "If something seems too good to be true, it probably is."

It turns out we did have a deal, of sorts, a deal that fell through because somebody at the record company got cold feet about our sound—*they're not grunge, we want grunge, grunge sells*—or about our name, yeah, yeah, yeah, we have a crazy name. But we have a *deal.* So, deal with it. Our side negotiates a settlement, resulting in enough cash to rent a recording studio in Charlotte, hire an engineer and a producer, so we can actually cut a record. We don't have enough cash for a full twelve-song album so we decide to put together a five-song EP.

We go with our two surefire cuts—"Only Wanna Be With You" and "Hold My Hand." We add "Old Man & Me," a song that we all believe should be a hit, and we include two new songs, "If You're Going My Way" and "Sorry's Not Enough."

"Our first album," somebody says one night, late, after a recording session.

"Well, our first EP," somebody corrects.

"Our first record," somebody else says.

We're high, or drunk, and we're all happy, content, spread out in a living room, watching comedians doing stand-up on Comedy Central as we all chill out together.

"We need a name," I say.

"We have a name," somebody says. "Hootie & The Blowfish. Can't change it now."

"No, dumbass. For the *EP.*"

"Huh," somebody says. "Yeah."

Silence sinks over the room, the only sound coming from the TV as an unseen audience roars at a joke a comedian tells. I feel like I'm staring into a fog. I squint and try to focus on the screen, on the comic. A heavyset Black woman. Prowling the stage. Holding the mic. The way she talks is so familiar. So country. I lean forward. I recognize her now.

Shirley Hemphill from the sitcom *What's Happening!!*

She laughs at one of her own jokes and revs up to tell another. From North Carolina, Shirley speaks in a thick Southern drawl.

"These girls today, the clothes they wear, *shit*. They show everything. My sister bought a thong bikini. I told her if you wear that in public, you gonna have to shave your kootchy pop."

The four of us absolutely lose it. I'm hysterical. I roll on the floor, which amazes me, because a second ago, I was on the couch. I suddenly stand up.

"That's it!" I shout. "The name of the EP!"

"Yes!" Dean shouts, then says, "What is?"

"Kootchypop!"

A moment passes and then we all crack up again.

"I'm serious," I say, when we finally hold it together.

Another roar, another thunderclap of laughter.

"It is pretty great," Dean says, my second, my other half.

"I like it," Soni says.

"It's different," Mark says. "Nobody will ever know what it really means."

"I guess we just voted," I say. "Introducing *Kootchypop,* the first EP by Hootie & The Blowfish. Named after Shirley Hemphill's sister's snatch."

"It can't miss," Dean says.

12

"CRAZY OVER YOU"

Foster & Lloyd

*K*ootchypop.

Our first record.

We make hundreds of copies and send them everywhere, an epic CD blast, to record stores throughout the South, radio stations, record company executives, and to anyone we have ever met or heard of who's within shouting distance of the music industry. Then we cram into our van and hit the road for something like a dozen dates in a row—playing, partying, and hoping for our EP to hit, to catch somebody's ear. Waiting for *Kootchypop* to become a household word.

At one point, my brain fastens on a lyric from a Foster & Lloyd song, "Crazy Over You"—

Is there a chance of gettin' through?

The song is about a guy desperately trying to get close to a woman, but that one line keeps slamming around in my head. Then I think about the first time I ever heard that song.

A few years ago.

Nineteen eighty-eight or 1989.

I'm working at Sounds Familiar and I have a reputation. I'm the guy who's knowledgeable about all types of music and who, without exception, is always late. I can't help it. I keep sleeping through my alarm.

"I know it's hard to believe," I keep telling Sharon, my boss. "How can I be late when my shift starts at one?"

I actually have a good reason. We play late, then we have to gather all our stuff, drive back to town if we're on the road, and then I'm so wired that by the time I fall asleep, it's dawn.

I vow to change that pattern. One morning, I set my alarm an hour earlier. I roll out of bed, make a pot of coffee, pour a cup, plop down in front of the TV, and start flipping through channels. I land on the country music version of MTV. I don't arrive here by accident. I love country music and listen to it constantly. It's my go-to. I settle into my chair, sip my coffee, watch a couple of videos without much interest, and then "Crazy Over You," by a country duo, Radney Foster and Bill Lloyd, comes on, the single from their debut album, *Foster & Lloyd*. The song slays me. I chug my coffee, leap off the couch, take the fastest shower on record, throw on some clothes, and race to the record store—an hour and a half before my shift.

Sharon stares at me as I burst into the store. "Are you alright? You're way *early*."

"Do we have the Foster & Lloyd album? I have to hear it."

"We have one. You know the rule. You can't open it unless we have two. Otherwise, you got to buy it."

"I'm buying it now," I say. "I have to hear this album imme-diately, as in right *now*."

I rummage in my pocket for my cash, buy the album, and play it on the store's turntable. I listen to the entire album. I don't merely love every song. It goes way beyond that. The music wrenches me.

"I want to do this," I say. "Exactly this. I want to sound like that."

A few years later, after recording three great albums, Radney Foster and Bill Lloyd break up. I'm devastated. Foster and Lloyd seem inseparable, the ultimate duo. They're like Dean and me. You

can't have one without the other. Then Radney Foster releases his
first solo album, *Del Rio, TX 1959,* and my life changes. I have
always believed that I am a country singer. As a kid, I listened to
country music all the time. I dug Kenny Rogers, his honey-soaked
baritone layered with *cool.* I loved Willie and Waylon, of course,
outlaws, couldn't get enough of them, and my grandma adored
Charlie Rich. But at Sounds Familiar, hearing Radney Foster's
voice, his new, evocative collection of personal songs about his life
and his hometown, feeling so moved by his vocal interpretations
of those songs, the power of his singing, the pain he feels in each
note, each word, I think—

That's who I want to be.

No. That's who I *am.*

Radney Foster makes me hear *my* voice.

And as Radney finishes the album with "Old Silver," a five-
minute masterpiece that practically brings me to tears, I turn to
Sharon, and I speak with an urgency and ferocity that surprises
even me. "You hear that? I'm going to do that someday. That's
what I have to do. That is going to be me."

. . .

Eventually, as the money continues to roll in, we do give up
our day jobs. We spend our days now in preshow prep, meaning
playing golf or pickup basketball, and as it gets closer to show-
time, getting high—in my case, mostly mushrooms or acid. We
continue to drive our ratty white van to gigs, despite the increas-
ingly tight quarters. By now, the van has taken on a distinctive
odor, a nostril-stinging combination of beer, sweat, and smelly
feet. In addition to the four of us, our instruments, equipment,
and four sets of golf clubs, we've added a fifth human, Paul Graham, our tour manager. The van has only two seats in front so
the rest of us have to cram into the open back area and find a
spot on the floor. To make driving even more interesting, the

van barely has brakes. We take turns at the wheel. I usually pull the late, late shift, after shows, not the best idea because being drunk and exhausted, I tend to nod off while driving. Amazing we survive these trips.

On rainy days when we don't play golf, we look for a local Y. Mark, in addition to being the band's engine and a truly superlative guitar player, is a hoop rat. He's tall and tenacious and eager to take on any five who'll play us. At first look, when we walk into a gym, we may not scare anybody. We've got some height—Soni and Mark are tall—but Dean, Paul, and I look slow, old, and fat. You may underestimate us. That would be a mistake.

One day, Mark is itching for a game. We're playing a gig in Wilmington, North Carolina, at The Mad Monk and we find a YMCA not far from the club. We walk inside, our well-worn, scuffed basketball cradled against my side. At the other end of the court, laughing, screwing around, shooting silly trick shots and occasionally dunking just to show off, is a group of high school kids. A starting five. They're quick, tall, and smooth, and they have attitude.

I hate attitude.

Mark suggests we play a game. Full court. Five on five. The high school kids against us old, pear-shaped guys. First team to eleven baskets wins.

We play. We blow them off the court. We win 11 to 2.

We run it back, demolish them again. We beat these kids to a pulp. We're old, true, and some of us may not be in the best shape of our lives, but we can ball. Mark has skills and can bang with anybody. Soni came to the University of South Carolina to play Division 1 soccer. The young man is an *athlete*. Paul Graham, too, is a jock. He ran track in college and can flat out hoop. Dean—quiet, chill Dean—rebounds, passes, and sets ferocious picks. You run into Dean, you run into a brick wall. And I can shoot. I'm streaky, but once I heat up, I become unconscious.

We mop up the court with these kids. But right before the last game we play, I notice one of the kids on his phone. Moments later, the guy he called struts into the gym. Their point guard. The all-star. The Mouth. First, though, he shows off his handle. He begins dribbling—*whap, whap, whap*—with either hand, then crouches and goes all Harlem Globetrotters—dribbling between his legs, behind his back, then he darts forward, stops on a dime, and swishes a fallaway jump shot from twenty feet.

"I'm ready," he says.

For some reason, he picks me out as our team's spokesman. "Yo, old man, you ready to run it back? You wanna check me? Or you too fat to guard me?"

"Oh, *snap*," I say. "That's the best you got? *Old* and *fat*?"

"No, I got plenty more. You'll hear it all during the game."

"Can't wait for your wit."

The Mouth says that since we won the last game, we can take the ball out. He rifles a hard chest pass at me. I catch the basketball, trying not to show how much my hands sting.

We've held the court for close to two hours now. We've got time for only one more game before our gig. I catch Dean's eye and see that we both have the same thought. As always. We want to end our run today with a win. We want to shut The Mouth up.

The game begins and quickly becomes a slugfest, hard-fought, fast, intense. The Mouth is the real deal—great court vision, clever moves, a deadly shot, and hops. He scores most of their points. Doesn't matter. We—the old, slow, fat guys—destroy these kids, beat their asses by five baskets. The Mouth never shuts up, spews a continuous torrent of trash talk. The more he insults us, the more motivated we become, the more determined we are to score, to win. We came into the gym looking for a friendly and competitive game of hoops. Of course, we want to win. But thanks to The Mouth, we want to dominate.

We end the game with a flourish.

Dean steals the ball and drills a long bounce pass to me near the opponents' basket. I'm wide open. I take a couple of dribbles and drive to the hoop for an open layup. But I hear footsteps. Slapping the wood floor. Coming fast. In my peripheral vision, I see The Mouth bearing down on me. If I go up for a layup, he will fly at me from behind, block my shot, and make a statement, along with another stream of sophomoric commentary. I take one step toward the basket, fake a shot, and flip the ball behind me—a no-look pass—to Soni, who's burning downcourt. The Mouth soars by me, completely faked out, as Soni lays the ball gently off the backboard and into the net, for the winning score.

"That's game," I say. "See ya."

We head to the corner of the gym and start gathering our stuff.

"Y'all can't fucking *leave*," The Mouth shouts. "We want a rematch."

"Nah, man," I say. "We're done. We got nothing else to prove. Ain't nothing left for us here, bro."

"You scared of us, old man. You know you can't beat us again."

"Let me give you some advice, young man," I say. "Ever hear the expression 'He talks a good game'?"

"Yeah."

"Well, you don't. Stay in school."

. . .

After the Y, we check into our hotel, shower, and change for our gig. The whole time, we can't stop talking about our dominant play at the gym, replaying the highlights of each game, and how we shut up The Mouth. We're still on a high as we drive to The Mad Monk for our gig. I will sometimes use The Mad Monk to gauge our success, or at least our progress. The Mad Monk is a historic venue and one of the largest clubs we play. The first time we played here a few years ago, we drew maybe fifty people. I remember playing that night and feeling that every note I sang echoed off the back wall. The room felt cavernous. But the next time we played the Monk, and every time after that, the crowd increased. This night, as we pull up in the van, a line of people wraps around the building. We have sold out The Mad Monk.

Someone mentions the sold-out crowd and the first time we played here.

"Things have changed," I say.

At that moment, I have no idea how much.

. . .

After the show at The Mad Monk, as usual, we sell copies of *Kootchypop* out of the back of the van. And, as usual, we sell out. I lose track of how many copies we move, but by the frenzy of hands reaching toward us for the EP with the crazy name and crazy cover—an ink sketch of cats dressed up, playing instruments—and the money exchanged, I'm guessing we sell at least a couple hundred. And we don't just sell *Kootchypop* out of our van. We hit all the independent music stores in Charleston, Columbia, Raleigh, Charlotte, and Myrtle Beach, offering the EP to the stores on consignment. We find out shortly that these record stores can't keep *Kootchypop* in stock. At first, each store wants five copies, then they call and ask for twenty more, and then fifty, then a hundred. We keep printing copies and *Kootchypop* keeps selling out.

Then we hear numbers that make my head explode.

A few weeks after we put out *Kootchypop*, we hear that we've sold *sixty-five thousand* copies, all in mom-and-pop record stores and out of the back of our smelly van. Then the demand increases. Record stores want more copies. The EP keeps selling. At this point, we're not aware of any interest in us from record companies. We just go to work. We hit the road, put our heads down, and play, night after night, in front of sold-out crowds in packed clubs, ten nights in a row, twelve, everybody loving our shows, our music, everyone dancing, partying, having a blast, the audiences and us, all of us, every member of the band taking turns crowd surfing. We've become the number one Southern bar band, a must-see show.

Then, finally, we hear it.

A noise in the distance. People talking.

Rusty, our manager, gives us the word. Record companies have noticed us and are starting to pay close attention. They're asking about us. Every week, A&R (artists and repertoire) reps contact *Billboard* magazine and the bigger record stores in the South and ask, "Who's selling?"

"Nirvana, Hootie & The Blowfish, Pearl Jam—"

"Wait, wait. Hootie who?"

"Hootie & The Blowfish. They're a big local band. Huge in the South. They just put out an EP, *Kootchypop,* that's selling like crazy. Outselling Nirvana, Sonic Youth, everybody."

"Kootchy what?"

"Kootchypop."

"What is that, some kind of ice cream cone?"

"Probably. Yeah. I don't know."

"Send me a copy."

August 1993.

I call *Kootchypop* our kindling.

Two months later, our kindling catches fire.

On October 31, 1993, we sign with Atlantic Records.

13

"THE BIRD"

The Time, from *Purple Rain*

March 1994.

Our band, the four of us, and all the folks we roll with, the people who take care of us, our equipment, our stuff, head to Los Angeles—the San Fernando Valley, specifically—to cut our first full-length album.

We drive in a caravan, our ratty van sandwiched between a couple other trucks.

Yes.

Our band.

When I was younger, preteen and early teens, I wanted to sing, but I didn't want to be in a band. Then, I remember—

Our living room in Charleston.

I'm sixteen and just scored a date with my current crush, Stacy Miller. I have to borrow my sister's car and she's late, so I'm late to pick up Stacy. Not a good start, but we're going to the movies, and we're both excited. We're about to experience the film *Purple Rain* for the first time. I am obsessed with Prince. Who isn't? I have already made my career choice, or at least defined my dream. I want to be a singer. A solo artist. I want to stand alone onstage, circled in a spotlight, singing my heart out, releasing my soul. Al Green. Otis Redding. Marvin Gaye. Stevie Wonder. These are the voices I hear. The singers I adore. I want to be like them. I want to be one of them.

Then I watch *Purple Rain*. A scene starts and The Time comes on. They attack the stage. They launch into "The Bird," Morris Day, the front man, strutting in his shimmering gold suit, grabbing the mic, posing. He belts the song, with Jimmy Jam and Terry Lewis behind him, then they move forward, arriving on either side of him, forming a line, and as they sing with Morris, they all move together in time, bouncing, flapping their arms like birds, in sync, a band that's as fluid and crisp as a dance team. Their harmonies kill me. Their choreography thrills me. This band—The Time—knocks me out. Right then, sitting in the dark in a movie theater in Charleston, I change my mind. I alter my course. I rewrite my dream. Watching Morris Day and The Time, I think—

That's what I want.

I want to be in a band.

. . .

The negotiations with Atlantic take a while, months, but then everything seems to move at warp speed, and we've signed, we have a deal with a major label to record seven albums, and we're on our way to L.A. to record our first *record*. It doesn't feel real—and it feels beyond real. It feels crazy and right. Destined. It seems like it all happened so fast—and that it has taken forever.

In the back of the van, I stare at Dean. "What the hell are we doing?"

Dean, the quiet man, practically shouts, "Going to L.A., dude. Making our *album*."

"That's *right*," I shout back. "We're making our fucking *album*."

. . .

Tim Sommer, our man from Atlantic, sets us up in L.A. Tim's our go-to guy. Tim's the reason we're here in the first place. The key to life is timing. *Destiny*. If you believe in such things, which, as you know, I do.

Apparently, some months ago, Tim's boss hands Tim a copy of *Kootchypop* and asks him to give the EP a listen as a favor to a friend. Tim takes his time, but eventually pops in our disc, likes what he hears, and is intrigued. He wants to meet us. He comes to Charleston, where we're playing a club, one of our regular gigs, hangs out with us, does preshow Jägermeister shots with us, takes in the gig, goes nuts when he sees us play, shares postshow Jim Beam and whatever else we pass his way, and tells us, "I'm going to sign you."

"Right, Tim, good, thank you," I say. "We've been here before. We signed a record deal. How'd that work out for us? Not well. Fell apart. Don't bogart that bottle."

"I'm serious, man. I am going to sign you."

"Don't take this wrong," I say. "I'll believe it when I see it."

Tim ends up hanging out with us for a week. Either he's a glutton for punishment, loves our lifestyle, or really likes the band. As for his promise to sign us, what I don't know then is that Tim's boss—and close friend—is Danny Goldberg, the president of Atlantic Records. Tim doesn't influence Danny's decisions, but he does have Danny's ear.

Bottom line.

Atlantic Records—and Tim—signs us.

. . .

On a Friday in mid-March 1994, we arrive at our destination, a nondescript apartment building in the flatlands of the San Fernando Valley. The building, our home for the next two weeks, is a grim, two-story mash-up of concrete and stucco, reminding me of a Costco or a minimum-security prison. The record company has given the four of us two bedrooms. Of course, Dean and I share one. After settling in, I step outside to a tiny balcony and take in the view. Peering into a murky brown haze, I see a grid of similar concrete and stucco structures, big box stores, and other apartment complexes, home, I'm told later, to hordes of aspiring writers, actors, musicians, and recent divorcés.

The glamor of Hollywood. Just how I imagined.

. . .

The next day we meet up with our producer, Don Gehman, handpicked by Tim Sommer. Don is quiet, cool, and knows exactly what he wants. He comes with impeccable credentials. He produced most of John Mellencamp's albums, and even more impressively for me, R.E.M.'s hit album *Lifes Rich Pageant*. I immediately feel plugged into Don. He understands our sound—our mix of acoustic and electric, driving rock songs and heartfelt ballads. We incorporate rock, pop, and country. Musically, we're kind of a handful. But Don gets us. I like his vibe. He puts us all at ease.

Once we start laying down tracks, a couple days later, we work from nine or ten in the morning until seven or eight at night. We don't put in these full days because we have to. We want to be here, making this music. It's even more than that for me. Playing with these guys, I feel joy. Sheer joy. During one song, as I play rhythm guitar, I glance at my bandmates. I take them in—Mark, his eyes closed, shredding his guitar, singing harmony, his forehead furrowed in concentration; Soni, bobbing his head slightly, every flick of his wrist producing the power of a hammer or the elegance of a brushstroke; and Dean, my twin, *Any day now, we'll find our permanent bass player and you can move on.* I grin at Dean. He smiles back, having no idea why. It doesn't matter. We share private jokes that are so private neither one of us knows what the joke is. Doesn't matter. If one of us thinks something is funny, it's funny. We laugh in solidarity, in connection, in appreciation of each other.

We've come so far, and, finally, here we are, all of us, literally living our dream.

I have never felt closer to these guys.

. . .

At night, we unwind at a local pub. We've become a regular contingent of seven—the four of us, Tim, and two young women who attend our recording sessions, Tina Snow and her best friend, Gena Rankin—daughter of singer-songwriter Kenny Rankin—a terrific singer herself, and Danny Goldberg's personal assistant. We eat, drink, laugh, all of us becoming a sort of after-hours family.

One night, we talk about recording "Hold My Hand" at an upcoming session.

"By the way," I say, "who's going to sing harmony on that?"

"I can, I guess," Mark says.

"Yeah, good," Gena says. "Or I can get David."

"Who's David?"

"David Crosby."

"David Crosby," I say, tilting my head, scorching Gena with a look of severe doubt. "Crosby, Stills, Nash & Young. That David Crosby?"

"Yeah. It's kind of late tonight so I can't get him for tomorrow. Probably be the next day."

I look at Mark, Soni, and Dean. They shrug simultaneously.

"Okay, right, Gena, sure. You are so fucking with me."

"I am so not fucking with you."

"The man is a legend," I say. "Why would he sing backup on our record?"

Now Gena shrugs. "I don't know. Because I ask him?"

"David Crosby is a genius," I say. "He is not singing on our record."

. . .

Two days later, walking with an easy, natural, shambling cool, David Crosby struts into the studio.

I instantly stop what I'm doing. I'm stunned, and then I freeze. I become a statue. David Crosby approaches me. I nod.

"Hey," he says.

"Hey," I say. "This is fucking real."

David Crosby laughs. "It is."

At that instant, I know. We have landed. The four of us. Four scruffy twenty-somethings, wearing T-shirts and cargo shorts. A bar band from South Carolina marooned in a recording studio in a place some call Hollywood adjacent and *David Crosby* is about to sing on our record. Yes, I am in awe. Yes, I feel like I'm elbow to elbow with rock and roll royalty because I am. Somehow I keep it all inside. I don't gush about what a huge Crosby, Stills, Nash & Young fan I am. I don't trip over myself thanking David Crosby for singing on our record. I don't tell him that this is by far the biggest thing that has ever happened to us. I do say something lame, like, "Hey, great, okay, cool," and then, thankfully, before I say something even lamer, we start recording, and David Crosby sings harmony with me on "Hold My Hand." He really does. Afterward, we all kick back, hang out, talk music and the music business, we laugh, we have a blast, us and David Fucking Crosby. To this day, I still can't wrap my head around it.

. . .

We finish recording our album in mid–April 1994.

Twelve songs make the final cut.

Eleven originals, one cover.

We decide the order with Don Gehman. I trust his gut, lean on his track record. Go with a pro. Every time. We kick off the album with the punch and *whap-bang* of the drums, then the jangling *rip-rip-rip* of guitar as we launch into "Hannah Jane," an upbeat, catchy tune that every time we play it live, gets the crowd surging to their feet. The song reflects our signature sound and sends a message—"Come on, y'all, get up, get moving, get happy." That's us. Who we want to be. We know we're different. It's the mid-nineties and everybody's into grunge. The music world is into grunge. Nirvana. Pearl Jam. Alice in Chains. Soundgarden. A musical movement bred in the Seattle underground, a mix of punk and heavy metal, featuring distortion, screeching guitars, nasally vocals, whining songs of apathy, self-doubt, and social alienation—"Smells Like Teen Spirit," "Man in the Box," "Black." We tried dabbling with harder-edged songs. For a minute. We couldn't do it. Not us. We're not dark and rainy like Seattle. We're sunny South Carolina. We have a social conscience, for sure, and our songs can be deeply emotional. But at the end of the day and into the night, we're having a party, and you're invited. We're pretty much the opposite of grunge.

On the album, we follow "Hannah Jane" with three of our strongest songs—"Hold My Hand," "Let Her Cry," and "Only Wanna Be With You." I love all three of these songs. Couldn't pick a favorite. I hear them all playing on the radio in my mind, one after the other.

We then get personal and political. In the remaining mix of eight songs, not in this order, we do "Drowning" and "Look Away," two songs about race and racism, and then two songs I wrote soon after my mother passed—"I'm Goin' Home" and "Not Even the Trees." We close the album with a traditional spiritual, "Motherless Child," the only cover on the album, a less-than-one-minute emotionally raw outpouring of my feelings, a stark contrast to the way we started with "Hannah Jane," a full-band blast.

I can't get enough of these songs. I listen as if I'm hearing some other band, one of my favorites. I know I'm biased, but I love this album.

Tim reveals the release date: July 5, 1994.

"One more thing," he says.

We need a title.

. . .

We toss out a million suggestions. Nothing sticks, nothing fits, nothing works. Then one morning, we're all sitting around, listening to John Hiatt's evocative 1987 album, *Bring the Family,* and his song "Learning How to Love You" comes on. One of us—Soni or Mark—suddenly fastens on the lyric "cracked rearview."

Lightning strikes.

"That's it," one of us shouts.

We know immediately that we've found the title.

Those words sum it up perfectly for all of us—our journey, our point of view, our *lives*.

Looking into the past. Seeing what's behind us, visualizing the landscape, but seeing it realistically, not with the distortion or benefit of hindsight, and then acknowledging the imperfections, accepting the cracks.

cracked rear view

Three words.

No caps.

Perfect title.

. . .

We finish the album, we leave L.A., head back to South Carolina, and hit the road. I feel a letdown—we all do—from the high of recording our album, those electric ten- and twelve-hour days, being together every minute, literally living together, eating, drinking, laughing, playing music, then repeat, morning, noon, and night, for *weeks,* and don't forget, David Fucking Crosby—

We go on the road again, but even playing in front of packed houses, larger crowds than ever, rocking, rollicking, getting high off the music and the Beam and the beer and the drugs—man, how could we not feel a letdown?

But then I look into the future—a few months off—and I feel another rush. Another high. The release of *cracked rear view*. After eight years, the world will come to know us. At last.

. . .

"We got a problem."

Tim.

On the phone.

He sounds stricken.

"What kind of problem?" I ask, but I don't have to prompt him. Tim is on fire. He has to get this out. It's like something vile has gotten stuck in his throat.

"I played the album for F."

F.

The head of Atlantic A&R. A major force at the company. Second-in-command to Danny Goldberg. The guy you want on your side when your album comes out. No. The guy you *need* on your side.

"Tim, tell me."

"He didn't get it."

Tim pauses, like, forever.

"What did he say? His exact words."

"I don't know if you really want me to—"

"Tim."

Tim takes a deep breath. The words rush out.

"He said he didn't hear any singles on the album."

I blink as if something has flown in my eye. I can't believe this. This is bullshit. "No singles. Not 'Hold My Hand' or 'Let Her Cry' or—"

"Yeah. No."

"Bull*shit*," I say aloud, and then I say, "Tell me everything he said. I can deal with it. I've dealt with a lot of crap in my life."

"Okay, I'll tell you what he said and then I'll tell you what I'm going to do."

He exhales the words.

"He told me he wouldn't release the album and then he went to Danny and said, 'If you put out *cracked rear view,* you'll be the laughingstock of the record industry.'"

I feel as if I've been kicked in the balls. I swallow, try to digest this conversation, and I can't. My head starts to throb. I massage the bridge of my nose.

"Fuck," I say.

"Yeah," Tim says, his voice low, sounding far off.

"Okay," I say. "So, what's the 'what are you going to do' part?"

Tim's tone changes. He speaks now with determination, with defiance.

"I'm going over his head," Tim says.

I hear the change. A vocal detour. I hear Tim's commitment to us, to the album, to *cracked rear view.*

"I'm going to Danny," Tim says. "The album's too good."

"When?"

"The second we hang up."

"What about F?"

"He's wrong."

· · ·

I'll never know exactly what Tim says to Danny Goldberg, his boss and close friend, but I do know that Danny overrules F and *cracked rear view* comes out on schedule. But the album hits the stores and airwaves with a whisper, not a roar. It arrives with virtually no fanfare from the record company. We make up for it by holding our own in-store celebration at Sounds Familiar for family, friends, and fans, followed by a block party that lasts well into the next morning. At the end of the first week, thanks to Sounds Familiar and other mom-and-pop stores in the South, the album sells out. We have a smash hit! Well, at least locally.

Nationally, not so much.

Five weeks after the album's release, *cracked rear view* cracks the Billboard 200 at number 161. Previously, the record company had selected "Hold My Hand" as the first single. Good choice. But the song hasn't flown up the charts. Only a few stations seem to be playing the record. As in, someone says dejectedly, exactly three stations. The following week, the album stays stuck in the mid-100s on the Billboard 200. The week after? Stalled. No movement. Same spot, mid-100s. We hear grumblings from the record company. Votes of no confidence. Except for those few radio stations in the South that are playing our single, we hear radio silence.

Six weeks after our debut, I feel that we're Radio Nowhere. With our song and our name, the only stations that play us, occasionally, are alternative rock, those stations you find at the far ends of the radio dial. Obscure, unheard, *alternative*. That's our résumé. I feel that vote of no confidence from the record company, zero support. Silence. Crickets. I imagine F walking down the halls, cornering anyone who will listen, grinning: "I told you so." As for our single, "Hold My Hand," nobody wants to hear it. It's not grunge. Kurt Cobain has died tragically only a few months ago, and with the outpouring of emotion, grunge rules more than ever. Have I mentioned—we're not grunge?

Then the impossible happens.

Or as I call it—destiny.

. . .

Tuesday, August 30, 1994.

David Letterman, only two years into his late-night show, but already crowned as one of the kings of late-night television, drives from New York to his home in Connecticut after the taping of his show. Letterman likes to unwind by driving, and he enjoys listening to the radio while he drives. A song comes on the radio. A song he hasn't heard before. The music grabs him. He turns up the radio. Man, he thinks. *This song.* The song *really* gets to him. He pulls over to the side of the road. The song finishes. He strains to hear the name of the band. The DJ says it. Sort of a joke name. Dave laughs. He'll never forget that name. He calls the show's booker on his car phone. He tells the booker, "I want this band on my show now, as in this week."

We are that band and the song Dave hears is "Hold My Hand."

Rusty, our manager, calls us Tuesday night. He speaks so rapidly he seems out of breath.

"Letterman wants you on his show," he says.

"Somebody pranked you," I say.

Has to be.

Because—Letterman?

Impossible. We haven't sold any records. We're not on the radio, except for three stations, one in Columbia, one in Charleston, and one alternative rock station in Atlanta. We are so far off the radar that even radar couldn't pick us up. Nobody knows us. Nobody's heard of us. David Letterman hasn't heard of us. By the way, I love Letterman. We all do. We watch his show almost every night. He's offbeat, snarky, hilarious. Perfect company if you happen to be drunk or high. Which I happen to be, on occasion, meaning nightly.

"Letterman doesn't know about us," I say.

"He does. He heard 'Hold My Hand' on the radio. He went crazy. He wants you on the show. This week. Friday night, if possible."

Then, incredibly, I say, "We can't do it. We have a gig."

Then, even more incredibly, the rest of us *agree*.

"Yeah, we have a conflict," Dean says.

"We're playing Township Auditorium in Columbia," Soni says.

"We sold out the place. It's our biggest gig ever," Mark says.

"Guys," Rusty says. "Let me call the label. We have to figure this out."

The label comes through.

They pay for us to fly private, leaving Friday morning for New York City. We make a plan. We'll do *Letterman* and then fly back in time to perform at Township Auditorium.

Friday night, September 2, 1994.

Hootie & The Blowfish appear for the first time on *Late Night with David Letterman*.

I dress for the occasion.

I wear jeans, my lucky Monterrey Jack's T-shirt, and my cherished Miami Dolphins ball cap.

We take the stage. We're the last guests of the night, following a hilarious appearance by actor Kevin Kline. One minute before we go on. I stand on my mark, in the darkened corner of the set, the space the show sets up for musical guests. I rock on my heels, back and forth, back and forth, waiting, counting down, my hands sweating, gripping my guitar's neck tightly as I realize, *I'm nervous. I'm really nervous.* I shake my wrists, lower my head, and murmur, "You got this," and the lights come up on David Letterman, sitting at his desk, leaning on his elbows as he comes out of the break. He grins into the camera.

"Our next guests are one of my favorite new bands," he says. "Their debut album is called *cracked rear view*."

He holds up a copy of the album and continues, "I have a copy of it right here in the very popular CD format. Here now to perform a great song—"

Letterman stops, swivels in his chair, and looks off at us, right at me.

"Are you boys ready? Is everyone ready? Is Hootie ready?"

He faces front and center, and again grins into the camera. "Ladies and gentlemen—Hootie & The Blowfish!"

We perform "Hold My Hand."

Four minutes and eighteen seconds.

I remember not one second.

I know we kill it. I know we play our asses off. I hear raucous applause rolling over us, and then I see Dave bounding toward us, grinning, shouting, "That was great, that was just great, great," then beaming and holding up our CD, shoving the album close into the camera and saying, "Hootie & The Blowfish, *cracked rear view*. If you don't own this CD, there is something wrong with you."

What we don't know then is that beginning the following Monday and every night for the next year, David Letterman will say randomly, for fun, for good reason, or for no reason at all—Hootie & The Blowfish.

For the next fucking *year*.

The show ends, Dave vanishes, we pack up and hustle out of New York City. We fly private back to Columbia, where, incredibly, a police escort awaits us at the airport. We climb into our ratty van for one of the last times, and then the police escort leads us to Township Auditorium in plenty of time to play our gig.

Nothing will ever be the same.

"THE LADY IS A TRAMP"

Frank Sinatra

After *Letterman*, "Hold My Hand" starts surging up the Billboard Hot 100 singles chart and *cracked rear view* rises into Billboard's top fifty albums. We continue playing some of our favorite clubs in the South, but we add larger venues as well, and we set up a national tour. In December, we shoot our first video for VH1, for "Hold My Hand." Turns out we're naturals when it comes to the camera. Well, we don't have to do much. Just stand and play the song. But we're so laid-back and down to earth that everyone on the shoot loves us.

"You're so easy to work with," someone on the production team says.

"Hey, this is fun, and we're all about fun," I say.

Then, in late December, another milestone. We perform "Hold My Hand" on *The Tonight Show with Jay Leno,* the first of what will be eight appearances on the show. With cash flow flowing, we finally junk our ratty van and upgrade our ride. We buy a true, tricked-out rock band bus—a rumbling, rolling combination rehearsal space, living room, and man cave with leather seats, air-conditioning, plenty of legroom for us and our golf clubs, a state-of-the-art sound system, a refrigerator, and most important, a fully and always stocked bar, and functioning brakes.

We head into 1995 on a high. We plan our first European tour, eight cities, beginning in Amsterdam, ending in Bologna, a month overseas. Then, right before we leave, we get the word. The amazing word. The incredible word. A word, I admit, I had fantasized about.

Gold.

cracked rear view, the album that F, a top record executive at our label and major naysayer, had only seven months earlier predicted would make the label a laughingstock if they released it, has gone gold.

I don't want to call him and gloat. I really don't.

Well, okay, I kind of do, but, nah, not really.

Why not?

Because, man, we're just having too much fun.

. . .

The party never stops. Whatever you got, I'm in.

Booze. Drugs. Everything you can name, anything you can think of, and piles of it, tons of it, as omnipresent as air. We drink, we smoke, we sniff, we stockpile. We once purchase two garbage bags full of mushrooms for fifteen grand, cash, right there on the spot. We stuff the mushrooms into the freezer on the band bus. I calculate we've just purchased enough mushrooms for a year and a half. Another time, after a show, we're sitting around on the bus, Dean, me, and a bunch of people we don't know, and I say to the guy next to me, "So, what do you do?"

"Seriously?" the guy says. "I'm a drug dealer."

"What do you deal?" I ask.

"Some weed, mostly X."

"X," I say reverently.

Ecstasy. Coke.

Our middle names.

I try to appear casual to the drug dealer. "So, how many do you have on hand?"

"Maybe two thousand hits," the drug dealer says.

"What do you sell them for?"

"Twenty dollars a hit."

"What do you buy them for?"

"About eight dollars a pill."

"Excuse me," I say.

Dean and I stand at the same time and huddle by the door. We come to the same number at the same time. I return to the drug dealer.

"I'll give you thirty thousand cash, right now, for all of them," I say. "Fifteen dollars a pill."

The drug dealer laughs. "Right."

"Wait here," I say.

I go to another part of the bus and find our tour manager.

"I need thirty thousand dollars, cash, right now."

"What? Why?"

"You know why," I say.

Our tour manager brings me the cash within five minutes. I return to the drug dealer and hand him bundles of bills.

"Thirty thousand," I say. "Did I take too long?"

. . .

When do we partake? Day, evening, night, into the next day, always. Nonstop. We take breaks to play golf and music. What comes first, partying, drinking, and drugs? Or golf, performing, and music? Chicken or egg. I honestly can't say.

When did it start? In college. First came beer. Then Jägermeister. Our go-to drink. Everyone's go-to drink. A thick, heavy green-ish concoction with a brutal buzz. Shit's heavy, man. Tastes like cough medicine mixed with fifty-six herbs and spices, as promised on the label. We do shots, every night, all night. Then someone introduces a shot of Jägermeister laced with Red Bull, called a Jägerbomb. Awful. Amateur mixologists Mark and Soni go one better. They create a Bagger—Jägermeister mixed with Jim Beam, which makes me want to throw up thinking about it.

I graduate from Jägermeister and go solo with Jim Beam, which becomes my drink of choice. I love Beam. Love it. I also love beer. I will pop open a can of Bud right after breakfast, shit, sometimes *for* breakfast. On show nights, I'll polish off two six-packs of beer and a pint of Beam by bedtime.

When we land in Amsterdam, the weed capital of the world, we up our drug intake. We do everything within reach of our hands, mouths, and noses. We do it all. Except, for me, weed. Not yet. I'm not into the Devil's Lettuce even though here you find the highest-quality weed in Europe. Otherwise, we do full-course meals of drugs. 'Ludes. Mushrooms. Ecstasy. Coke. Pills. We walk into dressing rooms backstage or lurch through our band bus and enter what looks like the Garden of Drug Eden. Miniature mountain ranges of coke blot out coffee tables. Pottery bowls overflow with pot, pills, powder, papers. The drugs are as much a part of the room as the carpeting or wallpaper. We're young, crazy, rock and rollers addicted to fun. We don't say no. We can't say no. We dive in. We party. We go insane. We never, ever stop. Ever. I look back at what we inhaled, ingested, smoked, snorted, and swallowed, and I am honestly amazed that we made it out alive. Despite showing blatant disregard for our bodies, our minds, our psyches, and our souls, we survived. We never consider the consequences, the history, the danger, the odds. Hell, we laugh about it.

"We should be dead," I say one night to Dean.

"Definitely, dude," he says.

"The gods must be with us."

"Amen."

At the end of our European tour—in Madrid, maybe, or is it Barcelona? The cities all blur—a roadie, an older guy who's been around, a guy who's worked with a lot of famous British bands, pauses while packing up our gear onstage. He picks up a cable, begins coiling it around his forearm. He looks at me. I stand a few feet away, sipping a pint of Beam.

"I've been out with everybody," the roadie says. "I've been out with The Stones back in the day when they were off-the-charts wild. I went out with Led Zeppelin when they were really going. But, man, I'm telling you."

He shakes his head.

"I've never seen anybody like you all. Nobody. I've never seen anybody go the way Hootie & The Blowfish goes. You guys are *nonstop*."

Wow.

I nearly say thank you, but I catch myself. His message hits me hard. The roadie's not giving us a compliment. He's not impressed. He's not in awe. He's in shock.

. . .

When we return from Europe, everything explodes. The album hits number one on Billboard and stays at number one or two for weeks. We release "Let Her Cry" as a single, and follow that with "Only Wanna Be With You." We shoot an atmospheric VH1 video for "Let Her Cry" and start tossing around ideas for a third video, this one for "Only Wanna Be With You." We join one of our favorite bands, Toad the Wet Sprocket, on a national tour. We're so crazy popular now that the Sprocket guys suggest that they open for us. We shoot that idea down. It's their tour. We'll open for them as we agreed. We do, however, spend time sharing the stage with them.

We start playing amphitheaters, arenas, stadiums. We play Jones Beach Theater on Long Island, the Greek Theatre in Los Angeles. Radio stations nationwide now play our music constantly. In what feels like overnight, we've gone from obscure to ubiquitous. Critics pretty much ignore us, but the public adores us. Our record sales prove it. Our singles storm up the charts, but *cracked rear view* is a fucking tsunami. The irony is that while F and other executives insisted eighteen months ago that grunge would kill *cracked rear view,* it turns out that *cracked rear view* has killed grunge. Hootie & The Blowfish doesn't merely dominate the airwaves, we *are* the airwaves.

It's crazy. We get into a car in Memphis, heading toward a venue to do some press. I turn on the radio and "Hold My Hand" comes on. Pretty funny. We snicker. I press the "Seek" button for the next radio station. "Let Her Cry" comes on. The four of us laugh. Two of our songs in a row, on two separate radio stations. What are the odds? I hit "Seek" again. "Time" comes on. Now, we roar. I hit "Seek" once again—and I swear—"Only Wanna Be With You" comes on. We lose it. Four stations, four songs, all ours, all at once. As I laugh, a lyric from the great song "For What It's Worth" by Buffalo Springfield pops into my head.

There's something happening here.

What it is ain't exactly clear.

But, man, it is crazy.

. . .

We get together—the band, Tim, and a couple others—for a creative spitball session for our next video. Everybody loves the video for "Let Her Cry"—moody, evocative, artistic, black-and-white—but we want to go in a different direction with "Only Wanna Be With You." Something lighter, more fun.

In the meeting, somebody asks, "You guys have any thoughts?"

"I do," I say. "I want to meet Marino."

Dan Marino.

The quarterback of the Miami Dolphins, my favorite team. In my mind, Dan Marino is the greatest quarterback of all time. Brady, Montana, Peyton, all great, but Marino is the GOAT. Fight me. I'll argue with you all night long. Back then, for the video, it may seem like Dan Marino and us is a stretch, but it's not. The song mentions how the Dolphins make me cry when they lose. Okay, fine, I cry when they win, too.

"Dan Marino," one of the creatives says. "Anything specific you want to see?"

"Doesn't matter," I say. "I don't care what it is. Can be anything. I just want to meet Dan Marino. It's my dream. I meet Marino, I can die a happy man. But no pressure."

"I'll reach out to the Dolphins," the creative says. "I'm sure Marino's heard of Hootie & The Blowfish."

"Who?" Dan Marino says. "I mean, I think I've heard of them. But not really. I'm not a big music guy. Let me ask Jimbo."

Marino asks his close friend Jimbo Covert, an All-Pro tackle who plays for the Chicago Bears.

"This Hootie & The Blowfish band, they want me to do a video," Marino says. "Are they anybody? Should I do it?"

"Hootie & The Blowfish want you to do a video?" Covert says. "Fuck yeah, you're doing it!"

So, thanks to Jimbo, we get Marino.

The video turns out really funny.

We do a spoof of *SportsCenter*.

Totally logical. All we do is drink, get high, play music, and watch sports. We're not casually into sports. We're sports junkies and we're addicted to *SportsCenter*. Then it hits me. We should do a video with all the *SportsCenter* anchors—Dan Patrick, Keith Olbermann, Chris Berman, Charley Steiner, and Mike Tirico.

We reach out to them. They love the idea.

The result is the "Only Wanna Be With You" video, one of my favorite Hootie & The Blowfish moments.

When the video starts, you swear you've tuned into *SportsCenter*. The iconic *SportsCenter* theme music plays and then Charlotte Hornets stars Alex English and Muggsy Bogues, in uniform, jog out of a gym and run toward the camera. Then we cut to *SportsCenter* anchors Keith Olbermann and Dan Patrick sitting at their desks. After our introduction from Olbermann, Dan Patrick, evoking a well-worn sports broadcaster's cliché, says, "You can't stop Hootie. You can only contain them."

With "Only Wanna Be With You" providing the soundtrack, occasionally cutting to the band playing and close-ups of me singing, the video evolves into a slapstick montage of Dean, Soni, Mark, and me playing sports—badly. Very badly. We are complete klutzes. We play basketball, terribly, with a group of NBA stars. We play golf, horribly, with Fred Couples. At one point, I try to chip out of a sand trap. My ball hits a tree and ricochets back at me. Then, the topper. Dan Marino—Dan Fucking Marino—throws a long pass to *me*.

Which I drop.

I really don't want to drop the pass, but everybody convinces me that it's funnier if I do. Wearing an official Dolphins jersey, which I still have, I sprint down the field. Dan throws a perfect spiral, as you would expect, I don't break stride at all, the football lands right into my arms, and as directed, I drop it. Marino slaps his head in disbelief.

It is kind of funny.

The whole video is a blast.

The band really takes off after the video comes out. The video also propels *SportsCenter* to greater visibility, turning it from a popular sports broadcast to a television institution. Even better, Dan Patrick and I really click. We start hanging out and he and I become best friends.

I look back at the first half of this year, 1995, and I want to pinch myself. It feels insane. Life feels almost out of control. I often take a moment, chill, and shake my head. Take it all in. And breathe.

Sometimes I wonder if it will ever end.

. . .

Around this time, I make another lifelong friend.

Tiger Woods.

Hootie & The Blowfish have arrived. Our singles are selling very well, and *cracked rear view* is going through the roof. We're in demand. But even though we're playing much bigger venues now, we refuse to cancel the smaller clubs we'd booked before people heard of us, or, as we call it, B.L.—Before *Letterman*. We all agree. We will honor our commitment to these clubs. They kept us alive before anybody knew our crazy name.

We play a club in Ann Arbor, Michigan, and after the show we go to a cool bar, Rick's American Café. I'm sitting at a table, enjoying my Jim Beam, and I see a familiar face, a guy at another table. Young guy. Maybe ten years younger than me, which would make him a teenager. I know him but I can't place him. Then I realize who he is. I've seen him on TV—and on *SportsCenter*—playing golf. I'm sitting across the room from the U.S. Amateur Champion—Tiger Woods. He's laughing, his smile lighting up the bar. I have to meet him. I slug my shot of Beam and head over to his table. I apologize for interrupting, introduce myself, and ask, "Are you Tiger Woods?"

He looks embarrassed. "Yeah."

I offer my hand. "You're the best."

"You, too," he says, and smiles shyly. "I love your song."

We spend the rest of the night together, closing Rick's. After that, we stay in touch and shortly become fast friends. Hootie & The Blowfish play at his wedding, I sing at Tiger's thirtieth birthday, I sing at his fortieth birthday, I sing at his dad's funeral. As time goes on, he gets hit hard by life. He goes through so much, physically, mentally, emotionally, and somehow survives. I stick by him, through it all. One night, hanging out at his place, I say, "No matter what, you will always be the greatest golfer ever to play the game."

"And, Darius, you are, and always have been, the soundtrack of my life."

. . .

Fall and winter 1995.

My seasons of dreams.

Actually, that's not true.

The events that occur during these six months are so impossible to comprehend and so surreal that I could never dream them. But they happen. They are real. They are my fantasies come to life.

In September, we return from our national tour. We close out the tour with a huge show at a stadium in Columbia, a sort of homecoming. In my mind, we will always be a bar band, but we are now a bar band filling a stadium, and everybody— the thousands of fans on their feet—sings our songs along with us. Then on October 1, we get invited to join Willie Nelson, Neil Young, John Mellencamp, Steve Earle, and the Dave Matthews Band to play in the tenth annual Farm Aid concert. I don't remember making the trip. I just find myself standing on a stadium stage in Louisville, Kentucky, as if teleported through time and space. We play a set of nine songs from *cracked rear view* and Willie Nelson joins us on "Let Her Cry." Then we bring out Radney Foster. Yes. Radney Foster, formerly partners with Bill Lloyd, whose album *Crazy Over You* made me believe that I am, at heart, a country singer. The same Radney Foster who wrote "Old Silver," a song I obsessed over, the man who inspired me to say to my boss at Sounds Familiar, "You hear that voice? That's what I want to do. That's who I am going to be."

At Farm Aid, in front of a packed stadium and millions more watching on TV, I share a microphone with Radney as we sing his brilliant song "A Fine Line." Suddenly, for a flash, I'm not even here. I'm in the audience, watching the two of us, Radney and me on that stage, singing, harmonizing, linked together, occupying the same time and space. I have to blink myself back to reality. Later, Steve Earle joins us for a rousing version of "Mustang Sally," one of our concert staples, and Radney returns, banging a tambourine, and he and I again sing side by side and share a microphone. The song ends and we hug. I have so much to say to him, but I clam up. The words, the thoughts, the thanks stick in my throat.

"Hey, man, that was great," Radney says.

You have no idea, I want to say. *You have no idea what your music means to me.*

But I can only manage, "Yeah, man, it was."

. . .

We stay on the move, remaining in demand, playing gig after gig, night after night. At the same time, we keep writing. I feel motivated creatively. I want to make sure we add fresh material to our gigs.

It's not that any of our hits feel stale. It's just that time is a motherfucker. I don't want to get stuck in the past, even the recent past. And I don't want us to go through the motions, ever. We've been playing the songs from *cracked rear view* every night for what feels like years, because it has been years. We're committed to growing, to shaking things up, introducing new songs. Plus, there's already talk of a second album.

At the end of October, Neil Young invites us to the Shoreline Amphitheatre in Mountain View, California, to play at his annual Bridge School Benefit concert. I'm feeling a little gassed from the travel and the nonstop performing, but when Neil Young calls, you answer. And who else is coming? Only Bruce Springsteen, Beck, Emmylou Harris, and The Pretenders.

We perform a seven-song set, opening with "Hannah Jane" and "Running From an Angel" from *cracked rear view.* Then we introduce four new songs, "Fool," "Let It Breathe," "When I'm Lonely," and "Be the One." Not everyone loves this decision, including more than a few members of the audience who want to hear our hits. We play with our customary commitment and

energy, but I can hear an unmistakably lower decibel of enthu-
siasm when we close our set. I shake it off during the finale, everyone crowding the stage singing Neil Young's "Rockin' in the
Free World." This time I share a microphone with someone who
is slightly more intimidating than Radney Foster.

Bruce Springsteen.

I have a million things to ask him, to tell him, but I just sing.
We howl, we growl, we rock out. We harmonize. Yes. The Boss
and I, side by side, next to each other for the rock and roll world
to see. I sing my ass off while trying not to freak out.

. . .

After the concert, backstage, I hang out with another of my idols,
Chrissie Hynde of The Pretenders. I try to act cool, pretty much
succeed, I think, although while we talk, just shooting the shit,
I can't help thinking, Big hair, throaty voice, punk goddess, yes,
Darius, you are hanging out with Chrissie Hynde.

"Excuse me."

A couple of fans approach me. Two teenage girls.

"Can we get your autograph?"

Chrissie and I both smile.

"Sure," I say and I sign their programs.

"We loved the show," one of the fans says. "But we were hoping you would play your hits."

"Yeah, we really wanted to hear 'Hold My Hand,' 'Let Her
Cry,' and 'Only Wanna Be With You,'" the other fan says.

"Well, yeah, we wanted to play some new stuff," I say.

I can't tell her that we've played those hits about a thousand
times and we've gotten a tiny bit sick of them.

"Oh, okay, just wish you had played your hits," the first fan
says.

"But it was cool," the other fan says. "You guys are still great."

Still great.

Ouch.

They leave, clutching their programs, but I feel as if I have been reprimanded.

"Did you guys write those songs?" Chrissie asks.

"Yeah. We wrote all of them."

She nods, seems to be weighing what to say next. "So, why would you not want to play a song you wrote when it's a hit?"

I can't answer her.

"You have to remember," Chrissie Hynde says to me, "it's not about you, it's about them."

I know the conversation doesn't end there. I know we continue with small talk, leading to some laughs, and it's all great. But her words grip me by the throat.

It's not about you, it's about them.

After that conversation, a sort of gentle dressing-down from Chrissie Hynde, I become the king of playing our hits, and loving every song again . . . and again . . . and again. I vow, for the rest of my career, the rest of my life, as long as I can sing, I will sing the hits.

They—the fans—are the reason the songs *are* hits.

The reason I'm here.

. . .

The Chairman of the Board.

Frank Sinatra.

In November, CBS broadcasts Frank Sinatra's eightieth-birthday celebration. George Schlatter, the show's producer, enlists a star-studded lineup to perform famous Sinatra songs for Frank and his wife, Barbara, who sit at a table on the side of the stage. The performers include Tony Bennett, Bob Dylan, Bono, Ray Charles, Natalie Cole, Steve Lawrence and Eydie Gormé, and Hootie & The Blowfish. I'm not sure how we score the invite, but when I hear rumblings about the upcoming CBS special, I drop a series of not-so-subtle hints to anyone within earshot that I am a *huge* Sinatra guy.

When we get the official ask, George asks what song we want to do. Without hesitation, I say, "The Lady Is a Tramp." We go back and forth about the arrangement. The show's musical director assumes we want to do a rock, "Hootie-style" version of the song. He sends us a cassette with the arrangement. I have to hand it to him. Somehow they've managed to make "The Lady Is a Tramp" sound like "Only Wanna Be With You." Impressive, but I don't want that.

I call George and tell him I want to re-create the Quincy Jones arrangement from the 1966 live album *Sinatra at the Sands*. I want the song to swing, not rock, and I ask that Hootie & The Blowfish play backed up by a full orchestra. George completely gets it. One final touch. We want to wear black suits and fedoras.

Dressed in our suits, we watch the show from the green room. Performer after performer sings for Sinatra and Barbara, who sit on the sidelines, looking like two well-dressed deer caught in a car's headlights.

I watch Frank's face during and after each song. He looks bored as hell, half asleep, or completely pissed off. I swear I can read his mind.

I'm Frank Sinatra. I don't want to hear these fuckers sing my songs. Nobody sings them better than me. Why the hell am I even here?

Then the stage manager pops in and gives us a five-minute call.

We leave the green room, hit the stage, take our places, the dim mood lighting comes up—a solo guitar introduction, and I begin to sing—

"She gets too hungry, for dinner at eight
She likes the theater and never comes late . . . "

The orchestra cranks it up behind us. I lean into the Lorenz Hart lyrics. I give the song every ounce of my being. The orchestra roars behind us. I glance at Frank.

He's leaning forward.

I close my eyes, get even deeper into the song.

I open my eyes and take another look at Frank.

The Chairman of the Board is smiling and snapping his fingers.

He hasn't done that all night. For any song. For any singer. He has barely looked alive.

I dig deeper into the song—and Frank starts clapping along.

For nearly two and a half minutes.

Two and a half minutes of heaven.

We kill it.

Our band kills it.

The orchestra kills it.

I lock it down, lifting it up, polishing it off, singing—

"And that's why—that's why—the lady is a tramp."

The studio audience stands.

Frank Sinatra stands. He waves me over.

I speed walk over to him. We shake hands.

"Son," Sinatra says, "that was great."

I'm twenty-nine years old, my career has just begun, and I have just experienced the highlight of my life.

. . .

Singing for Sinatra.

A dream come true. So, what do you do when your dream comes true? You get another dream.

It happens three weeks later.

December 6, 1995.

The Shrine Auditorium in Los Angeles.

The 1995 Billboard Awards.

I don't want to do this show.

I'm fried. For the past year, we've played every show that we've been offered, back to back to back, nonstop, traveling literally across the country. I can use a break. But then one of the suits at our label strongly recommends that we perform at the Billboard Awards. He points out that *cracked rear view* is selling historically off the charts. "You guys are getting people to come into record stores like never before." He floats a number that makes my jaw drop—a million albums a month. Another suit corrects him. "Sorry, that's wrong. It's a million albums a *week*."

A million albums a week.

Mind-boggling.

Then the first suit tells us that *cracked rear view* is up for Billboard Album of the Year.

"It would be a good thing to do," he says.

"I'm not feeling it," I say.

End of conversation.

We're not going.

Until the first suit finds out, somehow, that Al Green is my god.

"If you go," the first suit says, "we'll get Al Green to sing with you."

I laugh. "Nice try."

"I'm serious," the suit says. "If you do it, you will open the show with Al Green."

I tilt my head, take in the first suit's face, dare him to blink, wait for him to crack. He seems serious.

"I'm dead serious," he says. "I swear on your gold record."

Don't know how he does it, don't know what he says, what promises he makes, who he has to kill or fuck, but somehow, someway, the night before the show, I find myself in a rehearsal hall with the guys, including John Nau, keyboardist supreme, who's become the fifth Hootie & The Blowfish band member, waiting for the Reverend Al Green to show up.

Then Al Green enters the rehearsal hall and I am struck dumb.

It's as if Elvis has walked into the building.

You could hit me in the face with a brick and I wouldn't feel it.

Al Green has come into the room.

My childhood has come into the room.

When I was a kid, I didn't dream I was Al Green. I *became* Al Green, singing his albums cover to cover, performing for my mom and her friends, pretending a salt shaker was my microphone.

And now I will be singing with him, with Al Green.

I feel numb.

We go through the rehearsal. We will open the show with "Hold My Hand" and then in the middle of the song, Al Green will come out from the wings and we'll go into "Take Me to the River," which I will sing with—AL GREEN.

Darius, be cool.

I am cool.

I'm beyond cool.

I'm ice.

We finish the rehearsal, more of a walk-through. Al is Al, great, beyond great, but I can tell he's holding back. I'm not sure what or how much, but I have a sense I'll find out during the show the next night.

We open the show, we rock "Hold My Hand," giving it our all, backed up by a gospel youth choir, thirty kids wearing robes, clapping their hands, singing their hearts out. We get to the middle of the song, and then we stop. Dean hits the bass line of "Take Me to the River," my stomach flutters, Soni and Mark kick in, and then Al Green walks out. He appears to be on some other plane. That voice. He's singing this song with a power and ferociousness like it's the last song he will ever sing on earth.

Then Al kicks it up a notch.

He struts over to the youth choir, singles out a young man, and starts singing with him. Then Al goes into yet another gear. He takes his voice higher, his voice trills, his voice thrills, and the audience collectively lose their minds, and as one, rise to their feet. The guys and I just keep going. We play past our time limit and the camera cuts to the host trying to break away for a commercial, but the crowd is too intense, too insane, so the camera comes back to us and Al Green. I want to pinch myself. This is not a dream.

This is real. I am singing at the Shrine Auditorium in Los Angeles with AL GREEN.

This is it, I think. Right here. Right now. This is the moment. I can finally accept it.

It's not the record sales. It's not the sold-out stadiums. It's not the Grammy nominations.

It's singing with Al Green that makes me truly feel that we have made it.

15

"BIG POPPA"

The Notorious B.I.G.

We're feeling the heat.

Feeling flush, feeling the love.

Though not from everybody.

It seems the more successful we become, the more criticism I hear and read.

Too light for rock and roll.

Too cookie-cutter.

Too country to be pop.

Somebody even calls us "nice guys, too nice," meaning that as a sign of disrespect.

We're too *nice*?

The fact is, we're being criticized for our success. I do my best to shrug off this shit, but I'm human, and nobody likes being called out, especially for doing what we do, being ourselves, playing our music, and giving our fans a good time at concerts while having a good time ourselves. We may not be critical darlings in some circles, but our records sell and that counts for something. Some might say that counts for everything. If you're willing to spend your cash on our records that's all the love I need.

Then, a little more love and validation come our way. We get nominated for two Grammys—Best New Artist and Best

Pop Performance by a Duo or Group with Vocals for "Let Her Cry." We have very little chance in the first category against the likes of Shania Twain and Alanis Morissette, and we have no chance at all in the second category against TLC and their megahit "Waterfalls."

Still, it's an honor just to be nominated.

Yeah.

Bullshit.

. . .

Dean and I buy a house together in Columbia.

A sprawling three-story mansion in the center of town. Dean takes over the top floor, I take the bottom floor, and we share the second floor because it has the kitchen, dining room, bar, game room with a pool table, and a tricked-out living room featuring the world's largest and cushiest couch and a giant-screen TV that takes up an entire wall. I always wanted to buy a house like this for my mom. I wish she could have seen it.

On the Fourth of July, Dean goes home to visit his parents. I'm too tired to go anywhere so I decide to hole up in the Mansion and spend the time alone, chilling. I make sure I'm stocked with enough Jim Beam to get me through the night and then I go out to Blockbuster and rent a bunch of videos. I'm about to check out when, as an afterthought, I grab a video called *The Show,* a documentary about hip-hop music, starring and narrated by Def Jam founder Russell Simmons.

That night, late, I pop in *The Show* and settle in to watch an hour and a half of live hip-hop performances. About forty-five minutes in, a behemoth of a young man, a kid, really, calling himself The Notorious B.I.G. launches into his song "Big Poppa." I sit straight up. It's like I've been struck by lightning. I say aloud, "Holy shit." I have felt this way only a handful of times in my life when I've heard a particular song or artist, and this feeling is happening now. This music—this emotion, this rhythm, this beat—is physically disrupting me. My heart thumps. My soul feels rearranged. "Big Poppa" and The Notorious B.I.G. hit me that hard.

I rewind the video and watch The Notorious B.I.G. again. And again. And again. I watch countless times. And then I crash. I wake up at 9:30 a.m., unheard-of for me. I usually wake up in the afternoon. But I'm not only awake now, I feel energized. I throw on some clothes, drive to Sounds Familiar, and buy the Notorious B.I.G. album, *Ready to Die*. I put the CD on in my car and blast the volume. As Biggie Smalls belts his lyrics, I feel punched in the face.

I haven't been listening to much new music lately since we've been spending our lives on the bus. We rarely tune into the radio. We listen to CDs, mostly alternative rock, country, and older stuff. I haven't really caught up with much rap. The Notorious B.I.G. changes that. *Ready to Die* devastates me. The man is a poet. Every track is a masterpiece.

And every song tells a story in Biggie's unique, forceful voice. The next week, when we hit the road again in our bus, I play *Ready to Die* for the band.

"I can't explain this, how this makes me feel," I say to the guys. "You just have to hear it. Notorious B.I.G.'s voice. His vision."

They hear it, too. The anger, the pain, the power. They all get it.

Well, I think they do. I hope they do. At least some of it. Because if they get this music, they get me.

Nobody speaks. We all listen. Then when The Notorious B.I.G.'s hit "Juicy" comes on and he growls the lyric *stereotypes of a Black man misunderstood,* I close my eyes and nod along, my eyes filling up, the song driving into my brain.

The Notorious B.I.G. is speaking directly to me

. . .

Months later, at an awards show—the Billboard Awards or maybe the Grammys; my memory blurs—I find myself in an elevator with a couple of guys from The Notorious B.I.G.'s crew and tucked against the back wall, Biggie himself. We acknowledge each other with a nod, but we don't speak. You never speak in an elevator anyway, but this time I want to break the silence. I want to tell Biggie that I think he's a genius and *Ready to Die* is a work of art. But I don't say a word. I'm struck dumb. We exit the elevator and almost collide with a gorgeous young woman who walks by us, causing the group of us to stop short and stare.

"Whoa, she is hot," one of the guys says. "I'll buy her a car and then she'll give me whatever I want."

Everybody laughs, and then I say, "Yeah, she's hot, but she ain't getting no money from me."

The crew roars—Biggie the loudest.

Two years later, I find out that Biggie actually remembered what I said in the elevator. A surprising and sad discovery.

In 1997, Christopher Wallace, known as The Notorious B.I.G., is murdered in Los Angeles in a drive-by shooting. He is twenty-four years old. I am so torn up, I cry for an entire day.

Shortly after his murder, Def Jam puts out The Notorious B.I.G.'s posthumous double CD called *Life After Death*. The album includes a song "Mo Money Mo Problems," performed by the rapper Mase. The song includes the lyrics—

Stay humble, stay low, blow like Hootie
True pimp niggas spend no dough on the booty

A shout-out, I realize, to that time when Biggie and I shared an elevator and checked out that hot young woman. The Notorious B.I.G. has given a response, of sorts, to the band's critics, especially those who think we're too "poppy" or "too nice." If The Notorious B.I.G—arguably the greatest rapper of all time—sees fit to praise me, Hootie, in a song for being authentic—that's validation enough. Even if I'm not Hootie.

. . .

On January 29, 1996, attending the American Music Awards, we receive another form of validation, this time from Garth Brooks. We collect the award for Favorite Pop/Rock New Artist and return to our seats in the vast Shrine Auditorium in Los Angeles. Moments later Garth Brooks steps to the podium to accept his award for Artist of the Year. Garth, dressed all in black, from his boots to his Stetson, considers his award, an impressive, gleaming black pyramid, and then pushes himself away from it.

"Thank you very much," Garth says. "So you'll know, right off the bat, I cannot agree with this."

A hush falls over the crowd.

Honestly, I'm a little drunk—all four of us are—but I'm pretty sure I heard that Garth Brooks has just turned down his award.

He lowers his voice. "Music is made up of a lot of people and if we're one artist short—"

Damn, I think. He hasn't written this out. He's riffing. He is speaking off the cuff, but from his heart—and it's true, he is actually turning down his award.

"Without any disrespect to the American Music Awards, or without any disrespect to any fans who voted—"

Garth Brooks takes a breath, places the award on the podium in front of him, dismisses it, and takes one slight step forward.

"For all the people who should be honored with this award, I'm gonna leave it right here. Thank you."

"He's talking about us," I whisper to Dean.

"Shit," he says.

"Shit," I say.

To remove any doubt, Garth Brooks confirms this in a press interview after the awards show. He stands calmly, flanked by a scrum of reporters who shove microphones at him, a semicircle of metal snakes, all lunging at him.

"Why did you refuse the award?" five reporters ask at once.

Garth tips his hat.

"I talked with a lot of music retailers across the country," he says. "They all said that Hootie & The Blowfish kept them in business. I felt that they should've won Artist of the Year, not me."

Sometime later, I ask Garth, a friend, about that night, turning down the award, and telling the world that we deserved it, not him.

"You guys should have won, no doubt, but Darius, you know where that award is?"

"I do not."

"On my mantel," he says, laughing.

. . .

A month later, almost to the day, we return to the Shrine Auditorium in Los Angeles for the 1996 Grammy Awards. We have been asked to perform and I lobby for "I'm Going Home," a song from *cracked rear view* that I wrote about my mother. The guys agree. We're up for two awards—Best New Artist, and Best Pop Performance by a Duo or Group with Vocals, for "Let Her Cry." I've reconsidered our odds and determined that we do have an outside shot to win Best New Artist but less than zero chance for the other Grammy. We have no control either way. But we can control how we perform. If we lose, show the world what they missed, I think, as we take the stage.

To be brutally honest, we have been drinking all day. We are *lit*.

Ellen DeGeneres, the host, introduces us, the lights come up, we go into the intro for "I'm Going Home," the guys play their asses off, and I sing the *shit* out of that song. The audience goes wild.

Take that, I think. It doesn't matter if we lose.

Shock.

We win—Best New Artist.

I'm feel like I'm floating as I somehow make it back onto the stage. I sort of blend into the background as Mark and Soni speak—a lot—for all of us. Leaving the stage, I mutter, "Thank you," and as security hustles us back to our seats, I say to Dean, to the room, to myself, "What just happened?"

Shortly after—it seems almost immediately—an odd pairing, Tupac Shakur and KISS, in full makeup and costume, take the stage to present the award for Best Pop Performance by a Duo or Group with Vocals. I'm suddenly whisked back to my childhood. I'm ten years old, standing in front of a mirror, KISS blasting on my cassette player. I stack three cans of peas and lay a flashlight on top of the pile to create my make-believe microphone. I grab a broom, twirl it, slash it, pretending it's my guitar, and I sing every song along with Paul and Gene and Peter. I wail and practically cry as I sing "Beth," drowning out Peter Criss, making the song my own. I channel him. I become him. I idolize all these guys. I love that they are so out there, so bold, so over the top. But mainly I love their music. And now, in this mammoth, ornate auditorium, as they surround Tupac, I stare at them, mesmerized.

I hear Tupac's voice in the distance, muffled, saying, "And the winner is, oh yeah—my homeboys—Hootie & The Blowfish," and I'm vaguely aware of a hand gripping my elbow, Dean, trying to pull me out of my seat. I haven't even been paying attention. I've been staring at KISS. I blink at Dean. I can't speak, but in my head, I hear, *We didn't win, did we? TLC and "Waterfalls" won, right? No? NO.*

I head back to the stage, trailing the others, swallowing, thinking, I'm about to meet KISS, to shake their hands, and Tupac is grinning and offering us our Grammy, but before I can get to it, Gene Simmons, towering over me in his twelve-inch platform boots, reaches down and pinches my cheek.

Gene Simmons pinches my cheek.

Call me a deranged, crazed fan, but I may never wash my face again.

We leave the stage, stumbling back to our seats, stunned, drunk, and in my case, possibly dreaming.

I have met KISS.

Or I dreamed I met KISS.

Somebody wake me up.

No, don't.

. . .

The Four Seasons.

The Grammy after-party.

A packed room. High ceilings. Floor-to-ceiling mirrors everywhere. Dim, smoky mood lighting. Opulence. Elegance.

We sit at the bar, the four of us, drinking shots and beers.

We're in a state of disbelief, exuberance, confusion, thankfulness, and celebration. We've won two Grammys. We've arrived.

At a table behind us, I hear a commotion.

Shouting, chairs scraping the floor, fists pounding a table. A female voice shrieking above the din of the crowd, carrying through the restaurant.

"Seven fucking nominations and you couldn't get us one fucking Grammy?"

I don't want to look. But I can tell it's one of the TLC women screaming at a manager or agent or record company suit. I noticed them when we came in. I sort of snaked by them, ducked my head to avoid being seen, and sneaked over to the bar. Now, though, she raises her voice even more and her shriek becomes a screech. "Not one fucking *Grammy!*"

Man, I hope she doesn't see us.

In my peripheral vision, I see a woman's hand grab a glass tumbler and gun it right into a mirror. The floor-to-ceiling mirror shatters. People scream. The room erupts with noise. Then she fastballs a second tumbler into another mirror and shatters that one, too.

"That's fourteen years of bad luck," I say to Dean and nod at Mark and Soni. "We're out of here."

"Yeah," Dean says, downing his drink.

"Let's roll before she runs out of mirrors and starts throwing shit at us."

. . .

I'm psyched. We're booked to play the King Street Palace, formerly Charleston County Hall, for the third time, but this time we've sold out the three-thousand-seat auditorium. This arena, a former cotton mill, is a Charleston institution. Tommy Dorsey played here. Elvis played here, as did James Brown and Bob Dylan. Dr. Martin Luther King spoke here. The Ice Capades, the Harlem Globetrotters, and the Ringling Brothers Circus all performed here. But mainly, back in the day, the Hall was known for professional wrestling on Friday nights. I remember going with my grandma Rose, mostly in summers, despite the Hall's lack of air-conditioning. We'd sit in the suffocating heat of the auditorium, a sauna of general admission, sweating, standing, and shouting for Dusty Rhodes, Tiger Conway, Jr., the Minnesota Wrecking Crew, and the main attraction, Ric Flair.

This night, we're the headliners. Before we go inside for sound check, I linger on the sidewalk and stare at the marquee, which announces in big block letters: "HOOTIE & THE BLOWFISH." I take a deep breath. At times like these, I wish my mom were alive. I would have comped her a front-row seat and brought her backstage after the show to hang out with us.

We complete the sound check, and Mark and Soni take off while Dean and I sit down at catering. Could be the late night, but we're both starving. We ravage the snack table, gorge ourselves on doughnuts, bagels, leftover pizza, whatever we can find. We're ripping through bags of chips when I notice Dean staring past me, toward the door. His eyes have widened and his mouth has formed a frozen O. He looks as if he's seen a ghost. I follow his eyes and see a man approaching.

"I know who that is," Dean mutters. "Impossible not to know. He's older. But he's your twin."

The man walks over to us and stops. He shifts his weight uncomfortably. Nobody speaks. Finally, I say, "Dad."

I turn toward Dean. "Dean, this is my dad."

"Wow," Dean says to him. "I never thought I'd meet you."

My father dips his head. "It's been a while."

Fifteen years. I haven't seen you or heard from you in fifteen years.

I lock eyes with my father. I stare at him. Except for the difference in our age, the gray at his temples, I could be looking into a mirror.

Fifteen years of absence. Of no connection. Of nothing. My father. A stranger. He has chosen to remove me from his life. He has remarried. He has another family, another life. I feel pummeled by emotion. I could shut him out, the way he has shut me out. But instead, I make a decision.

I will be the bigger man. I can't say that I will forgive him, but I will allow him in, at least a crack. I will be—open.

"Yeah, Billy," I say. I call him by his given name because I have a problem calling him *Dad*. "It has been a while." I swallow, look down at the floor, then raise my head up and speak with as much kindness as I can find. "But, hey, why don't we get together."

"I'd like that," my father says. "Let's do that."

"We're going on the road for a couple days. Let's get together when we get back."

We exchange phone numbers. He stands awkwardly, continuing to shift his weight as if he's trying to find a solid spot on the floor. I stand up next to him and half reach for him, but I feel too weird, too distant, too wronged to hug him, so we shake hands, and then with the repeated promise that we'll get together in a few days, he leaves.

"Wow," Dean says.

"You said it," I say. "Fucking *wow*."

. . .

We play the Palace, then hit the road for a couple of dates. On this short trip, I go uncharacteristically quiet and keep to myself. Dean knows that seeing my dad has shut me down. I sort of hibernate. My mind crackles with different scenarios going forward with my father. What now? Has my dad really decided to bring me into his life? What will a relationship with him feel like? What will it look like? I laugh. What am I thinking? I have no relationship with him. I never have. I think about the few encounters, near misses, accidental moments when our paths crossed over the decade and a half in which I have not seen him nor spoken with him. I remember going to a bar in Charleston and having the bartender tell me, "Hey, your dad was in the other night. He was telling us all about you."

"He was? What did he say?"

"Not much. Just that he was on the road with you and the band, hanging out, helping with things, you know."

I don't know whether to laugh, scream, or cry. I try to keep myself under control, but my voice cracks as I respond to this total bullshit.

"He's lying to you. He has never been on the road with us. I haven't seen him in years. Literally years."

The bartender and the customers at the bar look shocked. I've crushed them. As I tell them the truth, I realize I'm hurting them. They love my dad. And why not? My dad is a local celebrity. He's funny, talented, cool, fun to be around. Everybody loves him. He's great. He's just never been great to me. He's never been anything to me.

As we ride the bus to our next gig, images over the course of my life come to me. Moments. Few, scattered. I remember—

I am six years old. My dad has come by our house for a short visit. Short, as in minutes. As he leaves, I follow him to his car, practically running to keep up with him. I don't want him to go. I want him to stay and hang out with me. Spend time with me. That's all I want. Time. *Be with me.*

I don't know why, maybe because I want something from him, I ask him for five dollars.

"Five dollars?" he says. "You want me to give you five dollars?"

I nod.

My dad pulls out his wallet and hands me a five-dollar bill.

"You're the five-dollar man," he says. "That's you."

My father rarely visits after that, about as many times as I can count on my fingers. And every time he comes, he goads me, makes fun of me, saying, "Hey, it's the five-dollar man," and then he hands me a five-dollar bill.

I take the money.

I take it, but I don't want it.

I want his time.

But if I don't take his money, I'll have nothing.

. . .

Another memory floats into my mind, a more recent one that I have tried to block because it jarred me so much.

A year or so ago.

We're booked to play the new coliseum in Charleston, a sixteen-thousand-seat arena built for hockey and concerts. We're set to perform for three nights, all sold out. We're playing the biggest venues in the country now, our album sales are going through the roof, Dean and I have recently moved into the Mansion, and we've all bought brand-new $100,000 BMWs. We tool around town in our gleaming new cars, just to drive. We're like four hot-shot teenagers, showing off our first cars.

This night, Dean and I park our cars and walk to the venue

together. We go to the stage door and head backstage toward the dressing room. As we walk, Dean suddenly stops and stares at a police officer who's on duty for the night.

"Look at that cop," Dean says.

I turn to the cop and now I stare.

"He looks exactly like you," Dean says. "It's scary."

"Insane."

I step over to the police officer, who has been eyeing me, too.

"Hey, man," I say.

The police officer blinks twice, and then we shake hands.

"You're Blue's son," I say. "You have to be."

"Yeah," he says.

"I'm—"

"I know," the cop says.

"You're my half brother," I say.

He nods. I can't take my eyes off him. We are nearly identical and about the same age, twenty-nine or so.

"How old—?"

"I'm thirty," the cop says.

I sigh. "I didn't know anything about you. I didn't know you existed."

My legs start to quiver. I feel as if I might fall over. I lean my hand against the wall to steady myself. I think I'm in a state of shock. I shake my head, my eyes still fixed on my half brother.

"We have to get ready for the show," I say.

"It's, you know, nice to meet you," the police officer says.

"Yeah," I say. "Sorry. This is weird. It's like I'm looking in a mirror."

"Crazy," he says.

I gesture at his uniform, and for some reason, I say, "I'm proud of you, man. I'm sure Billy—your dad—is proud of you, too."

The police officer nods. We shake hands again and then Dean and I go to the dressing room.

"The man is your fucking twin."

"I had no idea he existed," I say. "I need a drink."

"Me, too," Dean says.

I open a bottle of Beam and as I pour out two shots, I feel my hand trembling. I put the bottle down so I won't spill anything. I look at the label, a label I've seen hundreds of times—a red ribbon against a paper-white background—but right now it seems unfamiliar, as if I'm seeing it for the first time. I stare at it for a while until I feel myself calm down.

My father has a son my age. He has a whole family that doesn't include me. He doesn't want anything to do with me.

"I forgot to ask the cop his name," I say. "My half brother."

I lift the glass to my lips.

. . .

These memories shake me, and linger, but when we return from our short road trip, I determine that I still want to get together with my dad. I don't know what I want from him. But I feel something, and I suppose I want a connection with him. Why lie? I want a father. I know that's too much to ask. I know it's too late. But I'll take this opportunity and get together with him. We can start over. A step at a time. We can begin—something.

I walk into my part of the Mansion—the whole first floor—put down my bags, and check my answering machine, always the first thing I do after a trip. The red light on the machine blinks. I sit down at the kitchen counter and hit "Play." The messages start coming on. On the third or fourth message, I hear my father's voice. He clears his throat before he speaks.

"Darius, hey, son. It's your daddy. So, you know, listen, I got some problems, man. Financial problems. I got a lot of bills. I'm overdrawn. Can't keep up, you know. It's bad. I might lose my house. I could really use some help. I need about fifty thousand dollars. I know you can help me."

"Holy shit," I say to the answering machine.

I feel as if I've been slapped. I look up at the ceiling and I scream loud enough for Dean to hear me on the third floor, "Holy *shit.*"

I leap off my chair, and speak directly into the answering machine. "Are you fucking *serious*? I haven't seen you in fifteen years. I speak to you for five minutes, you tell me you want to get together, but all you want is my money."

I crack up. I start laughing uncontrollably.

"Awesome," I say. "You're a piece of work."

Then I remember when I was six years old and I stop laughing.

"That's right," I say. "I'm the five-dollar man. You gave me a five-dollar bill a few times when I was a kid and now you think I owe you. I guess those five-dollar bills really add up, huh? I now owe you fifty thousand dollars. Yeah. Makes total sense."

I look at the answering machine. I shiver.

"Awesome," I repeat.

Then I lean over and erase my father's message.

. . .

A few days later, I get up my nerve and I call my father back. I confront him. I tell him straight out that I'm not going to give him fifty thousand dollars. To my amazement, he sounds surprised.

"Hey, man, I'm not doing this," I say. "You actually leave a message on my answering machine, asking for fifty grand, when you haven't spoken to me in fifteen years?"

"I just thought, you know . . . "

His voice fades into silence.

"You thought what?"

He doesn't answer.

"No," I say. "Not happening."

I gently hang up the phone.

We never get together. We never hang out. He never calls me again. We resume our non-relationship. But Charleston is a small town, and I do bump into him a few times on the street. One time, while I'm walking down King Street, Charleston's main drag, a car pulls over ahead of me and stops. I look at the driver and see it's my dad, in a brand-new Cadillac convertible. He jumps out of the car and comes over to me.

"Oh, Lord," he says. "God is good. Thank you, Lord, thank you." He grips me in a clumsy hug, releases me quickly. "God has sent you to me, Darius."

"What for? What are you doing?"

"I'm test-driving this beautiful new car, I turn the corner, and, boom, there you are. God has sent you to me."

"You have to be kidding." I raise my voice and stifle a laugh. "If you think God has sent me to you to buy this car, you need to get yourself another God, because that is not happening."

My father seems shocked, or pretends to be shocked. He looks back into the car, at the car salesman sitting in the passenger seat, a stony-faced man in a rumpled suit.

"You won't buy me this car?" my dad asks me.

"No, Billy, I am not buying you this car, or any car."

"You sure?"

"Positive. As in zero chance. No way. Not now. Not ever."

"Okay, then."

My dad—Billy—stands military straight, sniffs, and retreats back to the car.

What is wrong with you? I think as my father drives away.

And then I ask myself—

What is wrong with me? Why did my father not want me in his life? I don't understand. I have tried to figure this out, but I simply cannot comprehend why a father would never want to see his child who lives in the same town, fifteen minutes away. *Dad, why? What did I do?*

I don't feel angry. I feel deeply hurt.

I decide to write about it.

The Notorious B.I.G. has opened my eyes, my ears, and my

heart. His music both lifts me up and tears me apart. For years, I have lived on a musical diet of country and rock. Thanks to Biggie, I have begun listening to rap and that has inspired me to return to classic and current R&B. I have also begun writing more songs, many of them deeply personal, some with a country tinge, others with an R&B flavor. I have even started toying with the idea of putting out a solo R&B album. A pipe dream, perhaps. But I can't help the thoughts and emotions that flood into my head. After seeing my dad on King Street, I go home and find myself hearing music in my mind, strumming chords on my guitar, and jotting down thoughts on a legal pad, which quickly become lyrics. Before I know it, I have finished a song about my dad and me, which I intend to put on my fantasy R&B album. I call the song "Where Were You."

Haven't seen you in fifteen years
And now you're walking through my life.
Where were you when I needed a friend?
Go away
I don't need you
Just walk away like you did before.

. . .

My father passes away a few years later. I don't remember who tells me. I struggle to remember any of the details. Or I don't choose to process them. I hear he's had a heart attack, or his liver or kidneys have shut down. I know he went into the hospital, his body failed, the doctors couldn't do anything for him, and he died.

I go to the funeral. I sit by myself, in the back row. I'm shocked but not surprised that my dad packs the place. His family sits up front, the family I never knew, his wife and a bunch of kids, including my identical-twin half brother, the police officer. My father's extended family attends, cousins and other relatives, some I know casually, others I recognize. Practically the whole neighborhood turns out, his friends, drinking buddies, dozens of acquaintances, coworkers, choir members. A few people speak, many of them professing their love for my dad, the man who fathered me, a man I never knew.

As the funeral ends, I try to get in touch with how I feel.

I'm not angry at him. I don't think I ever have been.

But I am sad. And I feel loss.

Billy—Dad—you're gone now.

You left me when I was six years old. You left a hole in my heart.

16

"COME TOGETHER/THE END"

The Beatles

In early 1995, we lose our champion. Danny Goldberg, our guy at the record label, the man who stuck his neck out for us, leaves Atlantic Records to become president of Warner Bros. Records. He leaves quietly, without fanfare, but to me, his departure feels seismic. Danny pushed *cracked rear view* past the naysayers at the record label. I also wonder how his leaving will impact Tim Sommer, the A&R guy who signed us, our day-to-day contact, and our other champion. I know this: I don't like change. I like stability. I detest uncertainty.

We don't hear from Danny at all until a couple of months later. He wants a favor. He asks if we'd be willing to include a Hootie & The Blowfish song on an album he's putting together for the *Friends* sitcom. "Anything for Danny," I say, and the guys agree. We choose "I Go Blind," which we'd left off *cracked rear view*. Later, during the *Friends* second season, attending a Hootie concert becomes a plot point for an episode and the song is featured. "I Go Blind" becomes a huge hit, with radio stations playing it for weeks, into the spring of 1996. I shake my head. Even though he's at a different record company, Danny remains our champion.

. . .

In March 1996, we're everywhere on the radio—AM, FM—and appearing, incredibly, on two record labels. On Atlantic, after being named the bestselling album of 1995, *cracked rear view* continues to sell, with "Time," our current single from that album, still going strong, and "I Go Blind," after playing on *Friends,* is a hit single on Warner Bros. In the middle of all this attention, feeling a surge of momentum, the four of us leave South Carolina and head to San Rafael in Marin County, just north of San Francisco, where we will meet Don Gehman in a large and luxurious studio and begin recording our second album. We arrive with a new batch of songs we've written over the past several months and a title we like, *Fairweather Johnson.* We all agree: *Let's put out a second album now, only ten months after* cracked rear view. *Let's take advantage of our heat. Ride the wave. Keep it going.* That's how we all feel.

Publicly.

Privately, the four of us have had intense conversations about the timing of the second album's release. That's not accurate. We've had heated arguments that have escalated into shouting matches.

Before the trip, I expressed my opinion, strongly and repeatedly.

I don't think we should put out a second album yet. I believe we should wait. I'm not gloating about our success, publicly or privately, but our first album—*cracked rear view*—has become one of the biggest-selling albums of *all time.* As in ALL time. We have passed ten million copies in sales and the album has generated four hit singles. The record company believes that we can release two or three more singles—maybe even four or five singles—which could propel *cracked rear view* into the stratosphere of album sales. The album would be our *Thriller.* The company projects that we could pass twenty-five million in sales, which would make *cracked rear view* the bestselling album ever. All we have to do is wait. Don't split the focus. Don't give the public two choices. They will keep buying *cracked rear view* because they will have no other choice. Record *Fairweather Johnson,* fine, but sit on it, keep it in the vault. Wait until later in the year or even next year when our first album's sales may finally start to lag.

I feel very strongly about this. Dean agrees with me. The suits at Atlantic are in this camp, too. They want to hold back *Fairweather Johnson*. But Mark, Soni, and Rusty, our manager, disagree. They think we should strike now and put out our second album as soon as possible. Saturate the marketplace, they argue.

Oversaturate, I think.

I see a fissure beginning in the band. Mark is adamant. He wants to release the second album *yesterday*. Dean and I vehemently disagree. Finally, we have to fight to get Mark to agree to hold off even this long. After we arrive in San Rafael, before we start recording, Tim Sommer, representing the label, flies out to try to talk us into delaying the release. He calls a meeting of the band. I am so not into having this conversation that I refuse to attend. I give Dean my vote. But Tim insists that he sit down with all four of us. I show up late and reluctantly. I'm in a mood. I'm argued out. I feel stressed and burned out at the same time. But I put a cap on my feelings and I go quiet. Because we want to show a united front and we don't want to give off any negative vibes or reveal even an inkling of disagreement within the band, Dean and I agree with Mark's position. We present solidarity. We say that we want to release *Fairweather Johnson* as scheduled, in April 1996, a month from now. I think Tim buys our unification act because he leaves the next day to pass on the word to the suits in New York. He returns with the band's insistence and this message—Hootie & The Blowfish want their new album out now. He has no idea that behind closed doors we've had dissension and shouting, resulting in a split decision, which was really no decision. For the first time, I feel a shift, a drifting away from all of us united in all things. I feel a splintering among us, a crack forming in the middle of the band. It feels strange. It feels sad.

But it's not new.

. . .

A few months before.

We receive an offer we can't refuse. Shit, it's more than an offer. It's a fucking gift.

Bon Jovi is playing Wembley Stadium in London, five nights in a row, fifty thousand people, already sold out. Bon Jovi's reps call us to open for them and play with them. A major get. No. *The* major get. It has happened. Bon Jovi can choose any band in the world to share the bill and the stage with them but they choose us. Playing this gig will propel us to a whole new level, something beyond superstardom. Game changer. Career changer. Done. Drop the mic.

Except we turn it down.

We don't go.

Soni has a conflict. He says he's sorry, but he can't make it. He has to attend a family reunion.

A what?

I ask because I'm not sure I've heard correctly.

He's turning down playing with Bon Jovi in England, at Wembley Stadium, because of a *family reunion.*

When I hear this, I think I go into shock. I feel as if my whole body goes numb.

A no-brainer has become a—brainer.

I seriously don't believe it.

I'm twenty-nine years old, and I search my mind to think of an event that would cause me to turn down playing five sold-out shows at Wembley Stadium with Bon Jovi.

Birth of a child?

No.

One of my sister's funerals?

Nope.

My mother's wedding?

I would ask her. I know what she would say.

Miss my wedding? Are you serious? Boy, get your butt to England. Go play Wembley Stadium.

But a family reunion?

Never. *Ever.*

We all have priorities and Soni puts his family reunion above the band and his career. Our career. Our future.

So, that's it. It's all of us or none of us. That's how we go. Who we are. We have given so much of ourselves to our work, to our music, to each other, we have sacrificed so much, put it all on the line, so many nights on the road, months, years traveling in that smelly van, playing our hearts out, killing ourselves, and now we see the culmination to all that, the payoff, the frosting on the cake—

Forget it. No use talking about it.

So we don't.

Looking back, that may be the most shocking part of all.

We do not talk about it. We simply accept it. All for one, one for all, all that shit.

Dean and I talk about it, of course. We don't say much. Not much to say, really. Neither of us can believe it. I do point out, quietly, that the week my mom died, I played three shows. I wouldn't allow the band to cancel our commitments. In this case, we let this opportunity go because we have to. If Soni won't play Wembley, then none of us will play Wembley. That's the way it has always been and always will be. That's the Hootie way.

I have learned that it's better to give in than to fight. Especially when I don't see a reason to fight. What would be the point? Nothing I say or do will change Soni's mind. I've learned that it's better for me to say, "Whatever you guys decide, I will do." Solidarity. In all things. It's worked for us. Well, until now.

I try to get in touch with how I really feel. I suppose I'm angry with Soni, but I honestly don't know if I am. I'm not really mad at him. I mainly feel—hurt. I wonder after all these years, are we still all on the same page? After Soni's decision not to play

Wembley, I'm not sure anymore. I do know that something has changed within me. Shaken me. Become undone. As a result, the dynamic of the whole band changes. It's unspoken, subliminal, but I feel it. We all feel it. And I know that we can never go back to the way it was.

. . . .

Something else happens during the eleven months between mid-April 1995 and mid-March 1996, before we head out to San Francisco to record *Fairweather Johnson*.

Well, two events occur, one that I love talking about, the other that I hate talking about because it guts me.

On April 21, 1995, my girlfriend, Sherry Ann Phillips, gives birth to our daughter, a beautiful, feisty baby we name Carolyn after my mom. I call her Cary, but every time I look at her, I see my mom and I conjure up her spirit, her intelligence, her strength. I hate being on the road, away from Cary, but I can't help the life I've chosen. The life brings fame, for whatever that's worth, and financial stability. Thanks to Carney, I honestly don't even think about money. But this life also comes with the cost of being away, constantly, and missing out on so much. I find myself trying to be a father from a distance. It's not hard. It's impossible. I beat myself up about it. I feel guilty and left out. From a distance, it seems that Cary's life is happening in a blink. She's about to turn a year old. Impossible. How did that happen? Where did the time go?

I deal with these feelings the only way I know how—by getting high. I've probably broken some sort of record for the amount of Jim Beam I've swilled over the past few years and I've paid for it by acquiring extreme stomach pain that a doctor diagnoses, in medical terminology, as a fucked-up liver. The doctor insists that I stop drinking or I will really fuck up my liver. I take his advice and I stop. For a solid three months.

. . .

The second event blindsides me.

Dean moves out.

I suppose I should have seen this coming. Every member of the band has a serious girlfriend. Mark has even gotten married. Dean has begun spending more and more time with his girlfriend, at one point even mentioning something about moving in with her. I hear that. I just kind of choose to ignore it. And I do get it. Dean wants to spend more time with his girlfriend. *D, she's the one. Soulmate. Want to build a life. Raise a family. Yadda yadda.* Okay, okay. Fine. But what about us? Dean and me. We're a duo. More than that. We're not even two separate people. We're extensions of each other. Two guys with one brain. Siamese twins.

He lays his decision on me so casually it's as if he's telling me he bought a new T-shirt.

"Yeah, man, you know, think I'm going to move out. Relocate to Charleston. Probably get married—"

I tune out. I don't hear half of what he's saying.

I nod and mutter a bunch of crap clichés.

Cool. Yeah. Great. Moving out. Uh huh. Nah. No problem.

Dean talks. I fake smile.

I try to pretend I don't care. I shrug like it's no big deal.

Inside, my heart screams.

My head pounds.

I feel obliterated.

Dean.

Every morning I wake up, shamble my way down to the kitchen, and find Dean there, always there, fucking up the coffee, eating some version of breakfast, watching sports, or listening to music, something new, or something we both love, an obsession like *Abbey Road,* our soundtrack. I hear that whole album in my head now, a mash-up, from the first song, "Come Together"—*He say, I know you, you know me*—to the sixteenth and last full song, "The End . . ."

The end.

Dean.

My brother.

The two of us. Inseparable. "I agree with Dean." "Dean has my vote." "Whatever Dean wants." Me and Dean against the world.

Dean.

My lifeline.

Dean.

No.

Losing Dean is like losing a part of me, literally. Like ripping off a limb. Worse. Like tearing off a piece of my soul.

He keeps speaking. I look at the floor. I can't look at him. I nod.

"No, I get it, man, you got to move out. I hear you. It's time."

Dean. Moving to Charleston. Two hours away. Feels like two time zones away.

"Charleston's great," I say.

"Your hometown," he says.

"My hometown. Yeah."

We say nothing else.

I keep nodding like a fool, pretending it's all good, everything's fine.

I'm lying.

I can't let him see that he has crushed me, that something inside me has died.

I just know—and I know he knows—that everything has changed.

Every. Fucking. Thing.

"Okay, yeah, so I wanted you to know," Dean says.

I am unfamiliar with that tone of voice. That inflection. That register. This guy doesn't even sound like Dean. He sounds like a bot. The AI version of Dean.

"Yeah, okay," I say. "Cool."

Silence drops over us like a shroud. We don't say anything for the count of ten, but it feels like we've gone quiet forever. I know that we've said all we will say. We're done. Got nothing left to say.

"So, I guess," Dean says, "I'll see you when we play."

I'll see you when we play.

Those six words.

Dean.

Stab my heart with an ice pick.

That's how I feel.

I can't say this is the end of the band.

But it's both the end of the beginning and the beginning of the end.

17

"SPEED OF THE SOUND OF LONELINESS"

Nanci Griffith

In March 1996, the four of us, with Don Gehman again producing, begin recording *Fairweather Johnson* in San Rafael. Physically I'm in San Rafael, but mentally and emotionally, I'm somewhere else. I don't want to be here. I miss Cary and, damn it, even though we're about to share the same recording studio, I miss *Dean*. He hasn't moved out yet, but in my head, he's as good as gone. So, basically, I'm in a shit mood. Crappy company. I keep my distance from the guys. They all stay in San Raphael. I book a hotel in downtown San Francisco, half an hour away. The first night, I check into the hotel, crash in my room, get obliterated on Jim Beam, and wait for Don to call me in the morning. I'm so over all of this that I don't want to see anyone before then. Shit, I don't even feel like singing.

Hootie & The Blowfish, I think, the words pulsing in front of me, blazing above me on an imaginary marquee.

I don't want to do this anymore.

That's how I feel. I don't say those words aloud. I don't act on my feelings. Instead, I brood, I simmer, I sulk, and I hide out in my hotel room. In the back of my mind, I think I know what I do want, what will snap me out of this funk, but it feels far-fetched. I have a longtime—I'm talking years—nagging desire to sing country music. That's what I want to do.

I want to make a country album.

Yeah. Me. A Black guy. I want to put out a country album. Charley Pride broke the color barrier first. He became a country star. I want to be next. Crazy? An impossible dream? Well, *cracked rear view*'s success seemed impossible, too. I can be Charley Pride 2.0. Why not?

Finally, of course, that's what happens. But back in San Rafael, in March 1996, as we're about to begin recording *Fairweather Johnson*, I'm somewhere else, far away from country music. Far away from everything.

The morning of our first day of recording, I call Cary before I head into the studio. I get her on the phone and talk to her softly, her adorable, babbling voice in my ear the sweetest sound I've ever heard. And then her mom, my ex-girlfriend, grabs the phone from Cary and begins screaming at me. She lights into me, going on a rampage, hitting me with a litany of my horrible behavior and inadequacy that causes my head to throb. She fucking destroys me, and then for good measure, slams down the phone. I seethe. I head into the studio, driving in a daze across the Golden Gate Bridge. I feel devastated. The second I park my car outside the studio in San Rafael, my outlook shifts. Now, I feel pissed off, irritated as shit. I walk into the studio, on fire, wearing my anger like a coat. I glare at every person I see: staff, sound guys, bandmates, Don.

Fuck all y'all.

I don't say that. I don't have to. But if you're within twenty feet of me, you hear it.

We begin the first day with a meeting. We sit around, the four of us and Don, talking about the album, the songs. Don leads the discussion. He's a calming, quiet, spiritual force. I love working with him although at this moment, based on my attitude, you may not know it. Mark, Soni, and Dean offer suggestions and comments. I say nothing. I stew. A few times, someone asks me a question. I shrug, or grunt, or answer in three curt words. Finally, Don ends the meeting. The other guys leave. I sit, shut my eyes, don't move a muscle. Then I start to stand. Don stops me, gently placing his hand on my forearm. "Hey, man, I got to talk to you."

"Yeah?"

"What's wrong?"

"Nothing."

"Nothing?"

"You're right. Not nothing. Everything. Every fucking thing. I am pissed off."

"About?"

I snarl. "About a lot of *shit*."

"Darius," Don says.

I exhale. "I'm fine, Don. I'm okay. I'm fucking good."

"Dude," Don says. "We can't do this. We can't make a record if you're going to be like this. We can't work like this."

I say nothing.

"I know you like your Beam," Don says. "You still drinking that all the time?"

"No," I say. "Only when I'm awake."

Don laughs, just a little, shakes his head, and looks past me into the studio's kitchen. A lanky hippie dude—the studio's owner, I think—stands at the counter, sipping coffee.

"Stay here," Don says to me. He crosses the room and approaches the hippie dude. "Hey, man, what's up? Any chance you can get me some pot?"

"I can get you an ounce or two," hippie dude says. "I'll get you whatever you need. I got a little bit right now if you want me to roll a joint."

"Oh, yeah, man, please. *Please*."

Hippie dude rolls me a joint and with Don urging me on, I smoke pot for the first time since high school. I get high and stay high for the rest of our time recording the album. I don't want to exaggerate, but I've been high ever since. After that first joint, my mood lightens up, I become more engaged with the guys, my work ethic kicks in, and I submerge myself in the music. I owe it all to pot. I smoke so much weed recording that album that we put a hookah in the control room. Now, when anyone asks me to name my favorite Hootie & The Blowfish album, I say, with no hesitation, *Fairweather Johnson*. Got to be. It's our stoner album.

Smoking pot pulls me halfway out of my melancholic hole. Then country music reaches in and pulls me the rest of the way out. Well, a country singer does.

Nanci Griffith.

I'm not sure who sets it up, but Nanci comes to San Rafael and sings harmony on two songs on *Fairweather Johnson*—"So Strange" and "Earth Stopped Cold at Dawn."

On "So Strange," with Nanci both backing me up and holding me up emotionally, I lower my head, close my eyes, and in full voice blast out of my funk. I kill this song, roaring these lyrics, words that engulf me—

It's so hard to breathe right now . . .

Ultimately, it will take a dozen years for me to realize my country music dream and career. But thinking about Nanci, I can pinpoint the exact day my country career began.

A decade before we record "So Strange" in San Rafael, I walk into work at Sounds Familiar in Columbia. As I head into the back to put down my backpack, I suddenly become aware of this voice. It's unlike any voice I've ever heard. It's sort of thin and high-pitched and plaintive, and absolutely fucking gorgeous. It sounds like a church mouse mixed with the voice of an angel. At this moment, the voice is singing an upbeat country song called "Mary & Omie" and I am floored.

"Who is this?" I ask.

"Nanci Griffith," one of my coworkers says.

I practically sprint to the turntable and grab the album cover behind it—*Once in a Very Blue Moon,* Nanci's first album, released in 1984.

By now, you know what happens.

I play the song once, I play it again, and again, and then I play the whole album, and then I play the whole album *again*. Then I rummage through our record bins, pull out all the Nanci Griffith albums I can find, and play every one of them—*The Last of the True Believers, Little Love Affairs, Lone Star State of Mind, Storms*. A few years later, I will become obsessed with Nanci's brilliant album of covers, *Other Voices, Other Rooms,* and go crazy over the John Prine song she sings with John himself—"Speed of the Sound of Loneliness."

After I devour all of Nanci Griffith's albums, her angelic voice practically lifting me off my feet with every song, I become fanatical about what certain FM radio stations call alternative country music, as opposed to traditional country music, which I also love, guys like Johnny Cash, Charlie Rich, Charley Pride, and Conway Twitty. In addition to Nanci, I listen to a slew of new artists, such as Lyle Lovett and his albums *Pontiac* and *Joshua Judges Ruth* and then I discover Dwight Yoakam and his records *Gone, This Time,* and *Hillbilly Deluxe.* I even get into bluegrass albums by the New Grass Revival, and completely lose my mind over Foster & Lloyd, and then Radney Foster, solo, especially his album *Del Rio, TX 1959.* You might as well inject that record into my veins. I can't stop listening to one song in particular—"Louisiana Blue." I hear myself in Radney. I want to sound like him. I sing along to his lyric, my voice going full throttle—*"I just want to disappear heading South a-way from here."*

I'm so insane over this stuff that I force-feed the music to the other guys as well, playing alternative country constantly and exclusively on the bus when we go on the road. I'm not sure if the guys love this stuff at first. But they indulge me and eventually they get into it. Except Dean. He tries but he never really digs country music, traditional or alternative. But the country music influence—even bluegrass—does appear on all our records, purposely or subliminally. It's prominent. You don't have to listen for it; you can hear it. I actually write "Old Man & Me" as an upbeat country song. In San Rafael, Don and the guys rearrange it, slow it down, making it more Hootie-like. I resist a little at first, but I give in and go their way. I always feel that we record our albums too slow. But I light another joint, get high, and go with the flow. In this case, Don's right. "Old Man & Me," the lead single from *Fairweather Johnson,* becomes a big hit.

I can't shake my country music habit. I start telling the guys, "I'm going to make a country record someday." I invite them to join me. "Hey, guys, let's make a country record next, after this one. All the way. Come on. Fuck it. Let's just go to Nashville and make a country album."

A few forced chuckles. A shrug, a grunt, a nod, a noncommittal smile.

"Okay," I say. "You didn't say no."

But, of course, they did.

Yeah, right, we should all go to Nashville and make a country album. Might as well ask them to record a rap album.

. . .

Fairweather Johnson comes out in April 1996. The album sells 400,000 copies the first week and shoots to number one on Billboard. Meanwhile, *cracked rear view* continues selling as well, sitting pretty at number twenty-one on Billboard, even after all this time. It's nuts. We've got two monster albums in the Billboard Top 50, three hit singles, we're planning a huge European tour, followed by a long American tour, and we're selling out stadiums. We're not just the biggest band in America, we are *omni-fucking-present.* We've hit the top of the rock-pop music mountain. We've gone as high as you can. I look up and I see nowhere else to go. Nothing but sky. And then I feel my neck craning, and the melancholy I felt in San Rafael returns. Instead of looking up into the clouds, I find myself peering over the side and looking down into a void, into oblivion. Suddenly, I feel my feet slipping on what feels like loose, shaky ground. The earth rumbles and then shifts beneath my feet. I'm going down. I feel it. I fucking feel it.

. . .

The slide. What I fear and felt happens. Just like that. In a blink. Sales drop, then plummet. In July 1996, two years after we released *cracked rear view,* and three months after *Fairweather Johnson* comes out, for the first time in two years, no Hootie & The Blowfish album appears on the Billboard Top 10. We're about to hit the road for the rest of the summer—our longest tour ever—and we all feel it. A change in the weather. First comes a feeling of shock, followed by malaise. A lack of energy. A dangerous, weird mix of emotions. A sense of concern blows through each of us, combined with a distinct sense of disinterest from our label without Danny's presence behind us. A hint of boredom. Then something troubling. A murmur of discomfort, disconnection, and sometimes dissension spreads through the four of us.

We tour, we play our music, we get high, we stay high, with pot my main means of escape. I don't want to face what I feel now, which is an extension of what I went through in San Rafael, during the recording of *Fairweather Johnson.* Then I begin to feel something else, something—*less.* Less excitement. Less hype. Less fun. Much less fun. By the end of the year and into 1997, I notice something else. Fewer people attending our shows. We still pack arenas, for sure—smaller arenas—but we're not filling up stadiums. I see empty seats. At first, I don't feel concern. I feel sort of—amazed. Then I begin to feel distracted. I start thinking about Biggie, his anger, his passion, his unique voice, and that motivates me, translating into wanting to express myself in my own R&B album. I think about my mother. My brother. My father. Those feelings start to consume me. I really want to do that, I think. I want to record a solo R&B album.

What about my country music obsession? Where does that go? Does it go away?

No. It goes deeper. Deeper than ever.

. . .

After singing together, Nanci Griffith and I become close friends. I love her intelligence, her emotional generosity, and her spirituality. She becomes my older, wiser sister. I confide in her, ask her advice, we laugh and cry together. I tell her how I sang her song "I Wish It Would Rain" over and over to my mother as she lay dying in her hospital bed. When I finish that story, we sob.

We talk about the music business, the insane life we lead. I confess my restlessness and malaise and uncertainty about continuing in the band. She listens and she hears me. She sends me spiritual books to read. I devour them. We discuss them. Because of our touring schedules, we don't see each other as much as I'd like to, but we talk on the phone constantly. One time, she invites me to lunch with an old friend. We meet up at a no-frills bar and restaurant and I take a seat across from a distinguished-looking guy with flowing white hair. Nanci introduces us.

"Darius Rucker, meet Harlan Howard."

I nearly choke on my beer.

Harlan *Howard*?

One of the greatest songwriters in history.

Among his dozens of megahits, he wrote "Heartaches by the Number," "Busted," which was recorded by both Johnny Cash and Ray Charles, and cowrote "I Fall to Pieces," sung by Patsy Cline.

I ask Mr. Howard a million questions, but I'm in such a daze I hope that I come across at least semi-coherent. Most of the details of that lunch remain fuzzy. I know I have more than one beer as does Harlan, and Nanci matches us beer for beer. At one point, I glance at Nanci and mouth, *This is awesome.* She smiles and nods.

1. Carolyn Rucker, my mom, my
heart. I sing every song for her.

2. Dressed in my football jersey, thinking about my
lifelong dream—to play quarterback in the NFL.

3. Posing center stage at my buddy Rick Johannes's birthday party, with his family. This was my home away from home. Rick's dad took me golfing for the first time.

4. Chilling, surrounded by my family, where I always want to be.

5. Early Hootie playing at a local bar. We're young, wild, and half of us are half naked.

6. Outside our ratty van, on the road to recording our first album. We're either hungover or trying to overcome the van's distinctive interior odor.

3. Posing center stage at my buddy Rick Johannes's birthday party, with his family. This was my home away from home. Rick's dad took me golfing for the first time.

4. Chilling, surrounded by my family, where I always want to be.

5. Early Hootie playing at a local bar. We're young, wild, and half of us are half naked.

6. Outside our ratty van, on the road to recording our first album. We're either hungover or trying to overcome the van's distinctive interior odor.

7. Launching into "Let Her Cry" early on. Check what I'm wearing—shorts, tee, ball cap. Typical show attire.

8. First Hootie & The Blowfish publicity shot. We look like we're suspects in a lineup.

9. Recording *cracked rear view* in San Rafael, California.

10. The 1995 Grammys. We won two awards—Best New Artist and Best Pop Performance by a Duo or Group with Vocal. I'm not surprised. I'm shocked. And thrilled.

11. Hootie & The Blowfish performing at the legendary Troubadour in Los Angeles. An intimate, magical evening. November 4, 2019.

12. Fronting Hootie before a packed house of 20,000 crazed fans at the PNC Arena in Raleigh, North Carolina. February 17, 2023.

13. Home can take many forms. Here's
one place I call home—a recording
studio, alone with my thoughts, and
my music. Always music.

14. Hanging with Ross Copperman, multitime
Songwriter of the Year and my cowriter on many songs,
including "If I Told You" and "Life's Too Short."
January 13, 2017.

15. Home again. Charleston, South Carolina. Getting the crowd to sing with me—even instead of me—always gives me chills. October 7, 2023.

16. Belting "Alright" in Charleston, my hometown.
Singing in front of my homies is better than all right.
October 7, 2023.

17. Rocking with my band at Ryman Auditorium in
Nashville to benefit St. Jude Children's Research Hospital.

18. My face says it all—pure love for country music. I am, at heart, a country singer.

Some months later, Nanci and I meet up in New York, where she's playing the Beacon Theatre. After her show, we hang out backstage. I mention her song "Love at the Five and Dime," which she'd performed that evening, one of her most famous songs and one of the most beautiful songs ever. I ask her if she's ever considered doing the song as a duet—with me.

"I haven't," she says. "I think it would be great. Let's run it."

Nanci straps on her guitar and we sing it, right there, backstage at the Beacon, the two of us, our voices connecting as deeply as our friendship. When we finish, we stand next to each other silently. I feel a crackle of electricity.

"Now, that was great," she says.

"Fuck yeah," I say.

We don't say anything else. We let it go. A beautiful moment singing together backstage at the Beacon. The end. But a few months later, Nanci calls. She invites me to meet her in London. She is about to record an album of her favorite songs at Abbey Road Studios with the London Symphony Orchestra. She would like to repeat our duet of "Love at the Five and Dime" and include it on her album *The Dust Bowl Symphony*. I fly to London on the next plane.

Recording that song with Nanci opens up something inside me. She has a unique voice, unlike anyone else's, and when we sing together we create a sound that absolutely stirs me. Something about singing a duet—the harmony, the sharing, the immense power of creating a third sound out of two unique voices. Singing *together*. I start listening to duets. I listen to "Love at the Five and Dime" several times, moved every time, and then I listen to Nanci singing, with John Prine, "Speed of the Sound of Loneliness" and "I Can't Help but Wonder Where I'm Bound." Country music. So deep, so personal. It's what I feel. Who I am. I will get there. Someday. Because right now, in the band, I feel stuck, as if I'm on autopilot, going through the motions.

You're out there running just to be on the run.

18

"BETH"

KISS

I n September 1998, we release our third album, *Musical Chairs*. We take our time writing and recording the material and it shows. I love how this album sounds, how it feels. We offer a variety of songs—a little bit of country with "Closet Full of Fears," bluegrass with "Desert Mountain Showdown," and classic Hootie rockers "I Will Wait," "Wishing," and "Only Lonely." Without a doubt, *Musical Chairs* is one of our strongest albums.

Nobody seems to care.

Sales start strong with the album hitting the Billboard charts at number four. But the record falls out of the Top 10 the second week. Six weeks later, the album drops out of the Top 100. As the album's sales continue to drop, we absorb other changes in the Hootie landscape, some hitting us even harder. John Nau, our keyboardist, leaves, a loss, but he's replaced by Peter Holsapple, a mandolin player and multi-instrumentalist master, a win. But then Tim Sommer, the Atlantic Records A&R guy who signed us, watched over us, guided us, championed us, and fought for us, departs Atlantic Records. A year later, in the fall of 1999, with *Musical Chairs* now out of the Billboard 200, we find ourselves playing arenas that are half empty. Shortly after, Rusty Harmon, our manager, leaves, and not on the best terms. Call it creative differences.

Overall, we feel shaken, and pretty much abandoned by Atlantic. The record company seems to have lost interest in us. Dean and I talk about this and express our concern and even anger to the group. We have done so much for the label. We've given the company one of the biggest-selling albums of all time. We've proven ourselves a viable alternative to grunge and brought customers back into record stores in droves. We've followed up our first record with two more excellent albums. They've sold well. They haven't matched the sales of *cracked rear view,* but only about a dozen albums in the history of recorded music have. To promote our records, we've worked the road tirelessly, touring all over the world, playing night after night after night. We've appeared on every television show Atlantic has set up for us and performed at every festival and fundraiser we've been invited to. We've never complained, publicly. We're not bad boys or difficult rock stars or prima donnas. We show up. We perform. We're still the fun rock band, *the* party band. It's just that in the end, we couldn't sustain that initial, insane, otherworldly success.

Weirdly, maybe all the work, commitment, and capitulation—being the nice guys, the good guys—has been the problem, the cause of the company to ignore us. That first year or so, mid-1995 through 1996, thanks to *cracked rear view,* we'd been everywhere, on every single fucking radio station. Maybe we should have held back a little. I know that we put out *Fairweather Johnson* too soon. Dean and I had that right.

I'm really not sure about anything else.

I only know that Hootie & The Blowfish remains a great bar band and that we have come to a crossroads.

. . .

In 1999, the record company throws me a bone. They encourage me to go ahead with the solo R&B album I've been clamoring to record. I write a dozen personal songs, all with an R&B and soul flavor, inspired by the likes of Jill Scott, Lauryn Hill, and Stevie Wonder. I call the album *The Return of Mongo Slade,* referring to an outrageous character played by Bill Cosby in a hilarious, obscure 1975 film *Let's Do It Again,* starring Sidney Poitier. An inside joke. I don't think anyone at the label gets the joke, but that's fine. Atlantic pays for everything, either as a thank-you for all the money Hootie & The Blowfish has made for the record company or because they believe in the album. Probably the former. I don't really care. *I* believe in the album and I think the record will sell.

The album doesn't sell. Not a single record.

The record company refuses to release it.

"We don't hear any hits," a record company suit tells me in a meeting before they pull the plug.

"What about 'Wild One' or 'Exodus'?"

Shrugs around the conference table. A company dismissal.

"We don't hear it."

I don't hear anything else the suit says. I'm livid. It feels as if the company has simply indulged me, allowed me to get my passion project off my chest without having any intention to release the album. A *fuck you*? A mind fuck for sure.

Finally, a year or so later, in what I would begrudgingly call a considerate gesture, the company gives the record back to me. I release the album two years later on Jill Scott's label, Hidden Beach. I'm proud of the album, which I retitle *Back to Then.* It doesn't sell well, but I don't expect it to. I've completed my first solo project and I prove, at least to myself, that I can go it alone, if it ever comes to that. Plus, I get to perform two incredible duets, one with Jill Scott, the other with Snoop Dogg. I love the record to this day.

Early to mid-1999.

Time blurs. Days and nights fold together. I can't shake my malaise. Can't seem to get a grip. I feel stuck in the muck of Hootie & The Blowfish obligations. "Bunch of bullshit," I mutter. We have a band meeting or two and I find myself disagreeing with the other guys, fighting over, I don't know, inconsequential shit. Shit that I want and they don't. Or stuff I don't want and they do. I'm the odd man out. The outsider. I'm testy, argumentative, possibly a dick.

The band moves forward and I go through the motions. Put on a fake happy face. As always, I rise to the occasion, get it up to perform. But otherwise, I'm no fun to be around. I feel like I'm in a deep slump. A rut. I let the feeling simmer. I walk around grumbling, mumbling, in a *mood*. I don't want to see anybody. I certainly don't feel like talking to anybody. But here we are, all of a sudden, marooned in the Hamptons, summer paradise of the East Coast, Gatsby land, performing at a fundraiser for President Bill Clinton. Big event. Open bar. Free booze. Thank God. This Hamptons pre-performance party I'm attending is overrun with celebs, movers, shakers, consultants, politicos, a who's who that feels more like a who's that? But don't go by me. This is power central. Money oozes. So much money you can feel it everywhere, hovering in the air, humming in the snow-white sand beneath your feet.

I feel out of place and out of sorts. I do not want to be here. I want to be alone. In addition to the band crap, I've broken up with my current girlfriend and while it's for the best, I'm a mess. I've been talking to Nanci nonstop. She's been keeping me sane. Don't know what I'd do without her. She gives me breathing exercises over the phone, reads me passages from spiritual books. I listen, I try, but I'm a lost cause. I cauterize my pain. I drink Beam and smoke weed. How does she even put up with my nonsense? Maybe some people see me as a prima donna. Jeff Smith, our tour manager, says the event manager thinks I'm, "her words, not mine, the biggest dick in the world." Yeah? So what? I don't care. Fuck her. Fuck them all. Man, I wish I could disappear. *Leave me the fuck alone.* That's how I feel.

You know what? I just decided. I'm not doing this fundraiser. Bill Clinton will do fine without Hootie & The Blowfish. I'm sitting this one out. Book some other band. I'm bailing. I crash onto a couch at the outskirts of the lobby. An hour later, five minutes later, I don't know, Jeff finds me comatose and curled up in a couple of couch cushions. He begs me to snap out of it, pull myself out of my mental quicksand.

"Darius, please," he says. "You're the draw. You're the reason all these people are here."

"They're here for Clinton, FOBs, 'Friends of Bill,'" I mutter. "I'm not an FOB. I'm an SOB. Haven't you heard? Wait. *You* told *me*."

"They want to see you. They want to see Hootie."

This pisses me off.

"I am not fucking Hootie."

"I know, I know, I get it. But you signed up for this. Come on. Let's do this. Come to this pre-fundraiser meet-and-greet for five minutes. Pretend."

"Three minutes," I say. "I'll come for three minutes."

I somehow haul myself off the couch and slouch into the main lobby, practically attaching myself to Jeff's side.

That's when I see her.

Talking, mingling in the center of a group of people. But I don't see anybody else. I can see only her. She's like a blaze of fire, burning into me.

She's tall, stately, and focused. She shakes her head and her flowing reddish-brown hair bounces off her shoulders. I can tell this right away—she's in charge. She exudes confidence and class. Wait. Is she the event manager who called me the biggest dick in the world? I laugh. The way I'm feeling lately, I'm sure that's her.

I find myself walking toward her. I'm drawn to her, pulled like a magnet. I approach her and I see now that, yeah, she's definitely in charge. She's really tall. Taller than me. Very put together. Elegant. I start to speak, but my mouth feels dry. I try to swallow. I need a drink.

Oh, by the way, she's also stunningly beautiful.

A fucking showstopper.

She turns her head and we lock eyes. For a split second. I blink. It's like the light off of her blinds me.

"Hey," I say. "How you doing?"

"Hi," she says.

"Darius," I say.

"Beth," she says.

Her lips wrinkle into a tiny smile. At that instant, something clicks between us. I feel it. I see it. She does, too. She has to. Then she turns away and even though she's right in front of me it's as if she's evaporated into thin air.

"I'm going," I say to Jeff.

"That wasn't three minutes. That was thirty seconds. You owe me two and a half minutes."

I grunt, walk over to the bar, and grab an unopened bottle of Jim Beam. "I'll be up in my room."

"Darius—"

I practically sprint to the elevator.

. . .

I stay in my room all night, chugging Jim Beam, finishing the bottle, then lying in bed, staring at the ceiling like a zombie. I can't sleep because I can't stop thinking about Beth. I have to see her again. I need details. I ask around the next day before the show. *Who is she?* She works for VH1. She's helping plan the event. *Is she single?* She has sort of a boyfriend. *Sort of?* That seems vague. I can deal with that. Nanci calls, asks how I'm doing.

"I'm hungover," I say.

"You sound it," she says. "But you also seem, I don't know, lighter. Not as messed up."

"Must be the spiritual books."

"Yeah," she says. "You're lying."

. . .

I spend a lot of time in New York so I can focus on recording my R&B album. That's what I tell everyone. It's true, partly. I primarily hang out in New York because Beth lives there, on the Upper East Side in a five-story walkup. I've made a vow to myself: I need this woman in my life.

When I first get to town, I call her and we have a casual catch-up conversation. We start with small talk, then advance to not so small talk. I hang up wanting more. I call her again a few days later. Then again, a few days after that. I ask her out. She says no. I wait a week or two. I ask her out again. She says no. I wait another couple weeks. I ask her out again. She says no, but there's something about the way she turns me down. I hear a tinge of regret. I think she's interested. Pretty sure. I don't give up. Finally, I wear her down, and we start hanging out, a lot, sometimes just the two of us, but she likes to include other people, often another couple she's close to. I'll take it. She doesn't mention the boyfriend, but I get the sense that he's still in the picture, at least to some degree. I've never met him and I don't see him as a threat. I see him as an annoyance. Then one night she calls me.

"I've got two tickets to the opera tomorrow night," she says. "*La Bohème*."

"Puccini. The music's unbelievable."

"Do you want to go?"

"Who, us? You and me?"

She laughs. "Yeah. You and me."

"Like a date?"

She pauses. "Yes."

"I'm in. I'll go wherever."

"Wherever?"

"Yeah. Wherever you go."

. . .

La Bohème blows my mind. An opera set in 1930s Paris, in the Latin Quarter, about four starving bohemians—an artist, a poet, a philosopher, and a musician. As Puccini's stunning music swirls around us, lifts me up, and digs deep into my core, I think that this story could be about the beginnings of the band and how the four of us struggled day after day, making music as we tried to make ends meet. A few years earlier, twenty-nine-year-old Jonathan Larson modernized *La Bohème*, creating the smash hit musical *Rent*. Both *La Bohème* and *Rent* end in betrayal, poverty, and tragic death. Hootie & The Blowfish have avoided all that. So far.

When the opera ends, I feel frozen, overwhelmed by the music, the emotion, and Beth.

We grab a taxi to her place and on the ride uptown, I feel a distinct change, an energy shift between us. As we get out of the cab and stand outside her building, I realize that we're holding hands.

"I thought you might like that," she says.

"I loved it. Every second. We have to do this again."

"I agree. I'll see what else is playing—"

"I mean, this," I say, looking at our entwined hands.

"This too," she says.

I don't remember if we kiss. I think we do. I know that before I can say another word she's gone, disappeared inside her building. I stand outside and wait for her to arrive upstairs, in her apartment, five floors up. After a minute or so, the light comes on in what I assume is her living room. For a moment, I picture her possibly imaginary, part-time boyfriend waiting for her, greeting her, hugging her.

I lose it.

"Hey!" I shout up toward Beth's living room window. "If anybody is up in Beth Leonard's apartment, you need to leave! Right now! *Leave!* Because I am going to marry her!"

I stand there, outside the building, staring at Beth's window. Beth, me, marriage. All we've done is hold hands and shared one kiss, maybe but I've never felt more certain of anything in my life.

. . .

Beth and I marry on December 9, 2000, on the beach in Bermuda. We decide on a small, intimate wedding, inviting only a handful of family and friends, fewer than thirty people in all. My three sisters attend and of course Mark, Soni, and Dean, who stands with me, my best man, still. Our wedding is exactly what we both want—no frills, a short, meaningful ceremony, an exchange of vows, and then a rocking beach party. As my dear friend Dan Patrick, says, "I was at a party and a wedding broke out." At one point, after Beth and I have been pronounced husband and wife, Charleston blue-eyed soul singer Edwin McCain and I surprise her by singing Stevie Wonder's, "Happier Than the Morning Sun," which is what I feel. I feel swept up by every moment, every detail of the day, but mainly I'm swept up by Beth, my wife, who appears celestial, showering light, as if she's the sun herself.

We settle into life together, a modern married couple. The businesswoman who turns heads with her intelligence and her looks, and the rock musician who spends three-quarters of his life on the road, making music and playing shows by night, getting high and staying high in the band's fancy tour bus all day. Beth and I manage the time apart as well as possible. But then we have kids—Daniella, born in 2001, and Jack, who arrives in 2004—and life as we know it changes. I parent as well as I can from a distance, which, frankly, isn't perfect. I am in awe of Beth, who juggles three roles efficiently and with grace—mom, wife, career woman. I don't know how she manages, especially as my malaise and unhappiness with the band and being on the road return. In the beginning, thanks to Beth, we survive. In the end, we stay married for twenty years, a testament to her in every way: to her strength, her resolve, and her commitment to our kids and to me. Sadly, we uncouple in 2020.

I can't save our marriage, but I will say, with all my heart, that Beth raises our kids and saves my life.

19

"LOUISIANA BLUE"

Radney Foster

We have fights, Beth and I, although most of them remain blurred by time and Beam and drugs, mainly cocaine. When I come off the road, I feel like a soldier returning from a battle. I'm bloodied and ornery and irrational and I don't want to engage with my wife or my kids or domestic life. I hate being on the road—and I can't wait to get back on the road and hibernate inside that tour bus. It's contradictory and makes no sense. And somehow it makes all the sense in the world.

I wear on Beth, I know I do. I make it hard for her. But I also know that much of what I say roars out of me due to cocaine's aftermath. She cries, I cry, I apologize, I swear I'll do better, and then I get high again and off I go, caught back in that vicious circle, not making sense. I feel sick and miserable and just shitty. After one epic scream-a-thon in the middle of another endless, sleepless night, Beth drops down calmly on the couch, puts her head in her hands, and says quietly, through tears, "If you could just stop being a fool and embarrassing me and embarrassing yourself—and just be a *human being*—I would make you the happiest person on earth."

I don't react. I can't respond. I don't know what to say. I don't know what to do.

. . .

The band—all of us, separately and together—feel stuck, and then angry. At the end of 2000, we release a passion project, an album of covers we call *Scattered, Smothered and Covered*. We record a bunch of great songs by artists we love, but who may be unfamiliar to some of our fans—Don Dixon, The Reivers, Vic Chestnutt, The Smiths. I particularly love the cover we do of the beautiful Tom Waits ballad "I Hope I Don't Fall in Love with You." Overall, we've gone with content over familiarity. Given the esoteric nature of the record, we know we need help in promoting this album, one of our favorites, but Atlantic does nothing. They ignore the record. They ignore us. The album makes a two-week cameo appearance on the Billboard 200 and then disappears. The lack of attention, the disinterest pisses us off.

We keep touring, but we don't book as many dates, and we don't fill stadiums the way we once did. We try to keep our heads up, our spirits high. But we all have families now, mortgages, car payments, school tuitions, so we keep playing, and besides, what else would we do? Personally, I continue to struggle to find my place. I never seem to want to be where I am. When I'm on the road, I want to be home. When I'm home, I want to be in the bus, on tour, playing music, singing in front of a crowd. Emotional whiplash. That's what I feel.

The months tick by.

Goodbye, 2001. Hello, 2002.

We commit to recording our fourth studio album. We decide we need a change. We all feel attached to Don Gehman. For me, he's like my spiritual guide, my guru. But collectively we believe we need a new producer, a new set of ears. We go with Don Was, one of the most successful producers in the business, who has produced albums for The Rolling Stones, Willie Nelson, Bonnie Raitt, and Bob Dylan. Don Was approaches us differently, almost as if he'd never heard of Hootie & The Blowfish. I don't know how he does it, but when we play, everything sounds brand-new. Don loosens us up. I really let go, channeling my inner Al Green, singing more soulfully than I ever have. Don somehow reconnects us, all of us, as artists, as friends. It's as if he discovers an unplugged wire in our creative circuit and reinserts it. We respond with a jolt. I have a blast recording this album, a collection of song treasures, including one of my favorite ballads, "Tears Fall Down." It's been years since I've enjoyed myself so much with the guys. We give the album a simple, spare title—*Hootie & The Blowfish*—because it feels like the essence of *us*. Atlantic releases the album—certainly one of the best we've done—on March 4, 2003.

It doesn't sell. In fact, it may be the lowest-selling album we've ever made.

. . .

After Rusty's departure, the biggest managers in the business call us, among them Doc McGhee, Bon Jovi's former manager. He wants to work with us. He's seen how we've been treading water at Atlantic and claims that he can help us, seeing a way to resuscitate our careers. I call Jon Bon Jovi for advice. Jon says going with Doc is a no-brainer. He says that if Doc wants to be our manager, you'd be an idiot not to go with him. Right now, we don't really have a manager and I don't want to be an idiot, so we hire Doc before the release of *Hootie & The Blowfish*.

During the release of the album, Doc mainly observes. He comes to two conclusions. First, we need to leave the label. We all agree. We still owe Atlantic several albums, but Doc makes a deal: we will allow Atlantic to put out a "best of" album in exchange for our freedom. We will be allowed to sign anywhere else we want. Second, Doc wants to target our touring. He presents a plan. *Don't tour just to tour. Tour smart.* He suggests we add corporate and private events, fundraisers, and increase our visibility in film and TV. Then, when we tour, tour strategically. Right now, we're working hard for the money. Too hard. We all still love to put on a good show. Great, Doc says. But put on a good show that pays, that makes playing your asses off worthwhile.

It takes some time, a year or more, but Doc's strategy works. He doesn't merely stop the bleeding, he starts putting millions back in our pockets.

As for recording, Doc sets us up at Vanguard Records, an independent label known for jazz, blues, classical, and folk. Doc, himself, has moved to Nashville, a city I love. I feel drawn to the country music vibe and the city's musical history. Doc also recommends that we go back to Don Gehman to produce. I love Don Was, but as a group, we feel a loyalty to Gehman. He started it all back in that studio in Burbank. He launched us. Of course, nobody anticipates a return to the success of *cracked rear view,* but we feel a new energy.

We record our fifth studio album, *Looking for Lucky,* in Nashville. I wouldn't call *Lucky* our best album, but I love the overall tone of the record. I still feel we record all our albums too slow, but this one gives off a distinct country vibe. Inspires me. I even suggest, again, that we consider putting out a real country album. Go all the way. The guys shoot me down. I'm okay with that. Never really expected them to buy into my country music jones. But I know that someday I will put out a country album, with them or without them. As for *Looking for Lucky,* it comes out in mid-2005, hits the Billboard Top 100 for a few weeks, and then fades. We see modest sales. Nothing special. Pretty much par for the course.

. . .

I'm a mess. I'm unhappy, I'm frustrated, and I'm high—on weed, mushrooms, and equal and excessive amounts of Ecstasy and cocaine. Tons of that shit. Tons. I stay high to escape, to avoid dealing with where we are as a band and who I am as a person, a husband, a dad. To be honest, I get high because I like to get high. I *like* it. A lot. I do. And I hate coming down. Coming down, I crash, I get cloudy, and then I can get moody. Translation: I can get mean. So I stay high. It's safer. More comfortable. I stay high to get by.

But when I'm with Beth, I disappear into myself, whoever that is, sometimes a guy I recognize, sometimes just an uncommunicative asshole. I do blame the drugs. Or my attachment to drugs. Beth deals with it. I don't know how she does it. But she holds herself together and holds our family together. She knows the problem—me. And drugs. She tries to talk to me. And when she does, I sense her fear. She's not afraid to talk to me, to speak to me from her heart. She's afraid *for* me, and for her, and for the kids.

Finally, she sits me down for the heart-to-heart I have been expecting and dreading. Still, I'm not prepared for what she says.

"I want to tell you something," Beth says. She takes a breath. "Before we started dating, I asked Dean if he thought I should go out with you. You know what he said?"

"Not sure I want to know."

"He said, 'If you want a good time, definitely go out with him. If you want to have a boyfriend, run for the hills.'"

"Deano. Yeah. I believe it."

"Yeah, so," Beth says. "Darius."

She studies her hands, her long, regal fingers entwined in her lap. She lifts her head and I see that her eyes have filled with tears. She speaks then with a hurt and fury I've never heard before.

"You can keep doing what you're doing. Partying. Doing all the shit you do. You can do all that, continue doing it, and I won't leave you."

My breath catches in my throat.

"Okay," I whisper.

"No, I'm not going to leave you." Then Beth raises her voice, slightly. "But I will spend the rest of my life—every waking minute—figuring out how to make your life fucking miserable."

I have been momentarily struck dumb.

"Stop partying, or I will make your life hell," Beth says.

She stands. Towering over me, she slams her hands onto her hips.

"Your call, Darius," she says.

The next morning I call a band meeting, only the fourth or fifth band meeting in the history of the band, and the first one I have ever called. We all hate band meetings. We call for band meetings so infrequently because a band meeting means only that something big has come up or we have a big problem.

I know what I have to do. It's clear. Radical. But necessary. I can no longer sit in the back lounge of the bus, watching someone put a mound of coke on the table, and all of a sudden say, "Nah, I'm good, none for me, thanks." Not a chance. If I see drugs and watch somebody dig in, I will go right in with them. Mark, of course, abstains, always has. He may drink a few beers, but he never parties like I do. I have told Mark what's going on, but I don't think he has a clue how heavy I go back there.

So, I call a band meeting and I get right to it.

"Guys, I need my own bus."

Deafening silence.

I know I'm asking for something unheard-of—I rarely ask for anything at all—but it's as if I've just confessed to a murder.

"Yeah," I say, to clarify, to emphasize, "I really need my own bus. The party is over for me. Beth's not happy. At all. That's an understatement. And I'm not happy. So, I'm going to stop going hard with the coke and the E. I'm going to go cold turkey. Stop all that shit. I have to. The only way I can do it is if I have my own bus."

More silence. I feel Dean looking at me, but I avoid his eyes. I stare at the floor and I mutter, "I'm fucking killing myself. I got to stop."

"Well, okay, this was unexpected," Mark says. "Let's talk about it later. I'll give my dad a call."

"I'm not actually asking," I say, looking at Mark, hard. "I need my own bus."

Nods. Grunts. Bodies shifting, guys standing, moving, nobody speaking, then everyone's gone, and I'm alone.

. . .

Snake.

What we call Mark's dad.

I love Snake.

Mark and Snake are close. Tight, as father and son as well as business associates. Mark consults Snake about everything, including all matters Hootie & The Blowfish. Everything. Every move. Every decision. Snake has a powerful voice, spoken through Mark. If I've said it once, I've said it a thousand times—Hootie & The Blowfish is Mark's band. I'm just the lead singer.

Mark talks to his dad about getting me my own bus.

Our tour manager calls me.

"Mark spoke to his dad," he says. "Snake emphasized that you guys are a *band*. You get paid equally and you split everything four ways, including expenses. Getting your own bus would be counterproductive to what you do, who you are, the four of you. Plus, it's an expense that we don't need right now."

"So, he refused my request," I say. "I can't have my own bus."

"Yes."

"Okay, here's what I'm going to do. I'll sing tonight, but you might want to call Corey Glover for tomorrow night. Or somebody else. Because I quit."

"Darius—"

"I. Fucking. *Quit.* I'm not doing this anymore unless I get my own bus."

I avoid everybody for the rest of the day. I take a nap before the gig. I dress for the show and head to the arena. I stop outside the building.

Parked by the stage entrance, I see our bus—and a second bus. My bus.

After the gig, I go to my bus, sip some Beam, one glass, and I crash. I don't know what's going on inside the other bus. I assume there's a party going on. But not here. Not in my bus. I don't do any drugs. I quit cocaine and Ecstasy that night, and have stayed away from those drugs for twenty years.

In my bus, I turn on the TV and mindlessly cruise from channel to channel, one single thought coursing through me, ripping into me, a terrifying realization.

I was one bad move from dying.

Thank you, Beth. You saved my life.

. . .

And then, it happens.

We come to the end.

Or at least our version of the end. Because the band never breaks up and we never will.

March 2008.

Right before our summer tour. The day before the tour begins, Soni calls a dreaded band meeting—number five or six, total, in more than twenty years.

His call for a meeting comes out of the blue. I have no inkling that Soni has an issue. I don't know what he wants, but I know something big has come up. Has to be. The only reason to call a band meeting. We hate band meetings.

We take our seats around the kitchen table at my house. After a few moments of uncomfortable, strained small talk, Soni begins talking seriously. Soni, we all know, has gotten sober, a complete turnaround for him. He'd previously been a record-breaking drinker and partier, a day drinker, even an *all*-day drinker. He has crashed and burned a thousand times, only to pick himself up and start partying all over again, every time. That's all changed, for the better. I'm proud of him. The Soni who has called this band meeting is a different guy.

"I've been doing a lot of thinking lately," he says.

He doesn't have to say anything else.

I know what he's about to tell us.

I could stand up right now, go over to him, hug him, and say thanks for the good times, thanks for being there, thanks for your thunder, thanks for your smooth and steady beat, thanks for always keeping perfect time, thanks for everything.

Soni speaks from his heart, but I'm gone. I've drifted away. None of his words land. Everything he says swims by me. My thoughts explode. A sort of dizziness drops over me. Here we are. The day of days. The moment that Hootie & The Blowfish has come to the end of the road, literally. We have reached the end of the run.

Soni speaks quietly, but with urgency, and absolutely no hesitation or doubt.

"I don't want to miss watching my kids grow up—"

I want to shut out the sound that's begun drilling into my head. I want the dizziness to stop. And then suddenly, I remember, all of it, every moment of the band's journey. I am back in college, singing in the shower, belting out "Honesty," and when I walk into the hallway, this guy Mark is waiting for me. That night we start playing together and we become a twosome, the Wolf Brothers. Dean joins us, then Brantley, he leaves, and we add Soni.

Dean, I think.

Dean, play with us this once, just this one gig, and then we'll find a permanent bass player . . .

We're still looking, Dean. Still looking for that bass player.

I see us recording *cracked rear view,* appearing on *Letterman,* beating all the odds, playing in front of packed, sold-out stadiums, winning Grammys, singing with Willie Nelson, Neil Young, Springsteen, Dylan, singing for *Sinatra*—

"What I'm saying is, guys, I need to stop touring."

Soni is speaking right in front of me, but his voice sounds far away and muffled, as if trapped in a canyon.

"I am definitely not quitting the band. Or saying that you guys should quit touring. And if you want to find another drummer, I totally understand."

"We'll never get another drummer. It's the four of us. Period."

Maybe I say that. Or Dean. Or Mark. Doesn't matter. We all feel the same way.

Soni clears his throat, nods, and says, "It's just that for *me*—"

For him.

For us.

What does this mean for us?

Soni looks at me then and says, "And Darius, I know you're hoping to dedicate some time to your country music project—"

My country music project.

My country music obsession.

Soni's right. I have been thinking about my country music project. More than thinking about it. I've written songs, made inquiries, but nothing serious or specific. I continually ask the guys to join me in Nashville, a lark, a fantasy. But they always say no. Dean turned me down the hardest.

I don't want to play country music, Darius.

I offered him three times what anyone else would pay him. We could hang out together, the two of us, like old times.

He doesn't want it. He doesn't want to play country music.

"So, yeah, I guess that's pretty much all I have to say," Soni says.

Silence. Feels like we're at somebody's funeral. I look from face to face and etched on each one I see what I feel—shock. Blindsided. We have arrived at this unknown place. It feels dark, unbelievable, unreal.

Nobody speaks for a long time and then finally, mercifully, we dive into details. Hootie & The Blowfish is a band, of course, but it's also our job. The source of our livelihoods. What will we do now? Somebody asks about keeping the health insurance for our families. Somebody else talks about dividing up what's currently in our bank account, splitting it four ways, and then talking to our financial advisors, wondering if we can live on royalties after our current tour.

I have these same thoughts, share these same concerns. But only briefly. I know that in a couple of months, when this current tour ends, reality will rap me in the head. But right now, another thought hits me, almost as hard as Soni's announcement.

I'm going to Nashville. I am going to make a country record.

I don't care if I get a record deal. I don't care if I record a bunch of songs in my basement on an MP3 player. I don't care if nobody notices me.

I hear Radney Foster's song "Louisiana Blue," his lyrics driving me—*I just want to disappear heading South a-way from here.*

I am going to Nashville.

20

"DON'T THINK I DON'T THINK ABOUT IT"

Darius

What am I thinking?

It'll never work. I hear the arguments against me. The negativity. All the noise banging inside my head, deafening, blocking out all other sound. Then I hear the explanations, the so-called reasoning, followed by a torrent of insincere apologies.

The country music world will never accept a Black country singer. And never a Black country *star*. Happened exactly once. Charley Pride. He made it big. He hit number one on the country charts. But that was twenty-five years ago. *Sorry, Darius. It can't happen.*

I float the idea to a few friends. They all have the same reaction.

A country singer?

No. No. *What are you thinking?*

. . .

I sit across the table from Doc McGhee, sipping a beer and picking at my dinner. Doc has chosen one of our favorite spots, but I'm not hungry. I'm antsy, anxious to move on, eager to explore life beyond Hootie. In the strangest way, I feel more energized, more motivated than I have in years.

"Let's talk about it," Doc says. "What are you going to do? What's next?"

I push my plate aside, take a moment, and say, "I don't know, Doc. But I'm going to make my country record. I really am."

I'm trying to act cool, but my passion blows through my words. I sound insistent, as if I'm offering Doc a challenge.

"You sound serious," Doc says.

I lock eyes with him.

"I'm dead serious. You know I've started writing songs. I'll finish them up, then I'll get some friends together and see what happens. I'm going to do it."

Doc says nothing.

"You think it's crazy."

Doc shrugs. "I don't know. Maybe."

I laugh.

A Black guy trying to break into country music. Nobody will take me seriously.

"*I* think it's crazy," I say.

Two weeks later, I'm home, chilling, half asleep on the couch, and the phone rings.

Doc.

I haven't spoken to him since our dinner.

"Hey, man," he says. "You still want to do that country thing?"

"Yes. I told you. I'm gonna do it."

"Well, good. I got you a record deal."

I sit up, instantly awake, not sure I've heard him right.

"Bullshit," I say.

"No, man, I mean it."

I'm still not buying it.

"Yeah, Doc, right. Sure you did."

"No, really, I did."

I massage my forehead. Something's not tracking.

"Doc, look," I say. "I appreciate you. I always do. But if you got me a deal with Joe Schmo Records, or some indie label, or something like that, I'd rather do it myself. I'll take my chances."

Doc either laughs or grunts or sighs. Hard to tell on the phone.

"Man," he says. "I got you a deal with Capitol."

I nearly shout. "Capitol Records?"

I'm stunned. Astonished.

"Yeah. I'm at dinner with Mike Dungan right now. Let me put Mike on."

Wait. Mike *Dungan*?

President of Capitol Records Nashville.

I'm standing now. And pacing. I pace across my football field–sized living room in two strides.

"Hey, man," Mike Dungan says over the phone. "How you doing?"

"Good, Mike, good."

"Darius, we're gonna make this happen. I want to get started right away."

"Great. I've been working. I've written a bunch of songs."

"Good. Let's get you into a recording studio."

Two days later, still in a state of shock, I fly to Nashville to meet Mike, go over the deal, and begin recording my first country album.

· · ·

Sometime later, Doc reveals the details of his dinner with Mike Dungan.

Doc doesn't meet Mike to talk about me. He meets Mike to talk about one of his other clients, Chris Cagle. Chris has had a long career in country music and has recently hit number three on the Billboard Hot Country Songs chart with his song "What Kinda Gone." I keep tabs on Chris. That song has not rocketed up the charts. The record has taken a slow, steady climb, inching upward, then after nearly a year, has finally arrived at number three. I credit Doc and Capitol for sticking with Chris, for never giving up on him, and for believing in the song. I want that kind of commitment and loyalty from my record company.

At this dinner, after talking about Chris and how well Doc and Mike work together, Doc says, "Hey, man, I got this guy. You got to give him a record deal."

"Who is he? Do I know him?"

"You know him. But I'm not going to tell you who he is until you promise to give him a record deal."

Mike Dungan laughs, and then stares, registering that Doc isn't close to kidding, and says, "Why the hell would I do that?"

Doc leans across the table, and whispers to Mike as if he's about to reveal classified information.

"Because I'm Doc Fucking McGhee. You have to say yes."

They get to dessert before Mike finally gives in.

"Okay, Doc, I'll do it. Based on your word, I'll give this guy a record deal, whoever he is."

They shake on it.

"Now, who is he?" Mike says.

"Darius Rucker."

"Hootie?"

"Yeah," Doc says. "Hootie."

Dungan takes a long pause, and then he says, "I never got the Hootie thing. But I always thought that guy was a country singer. Okay. Yeah. I'm gonna give him a record deal."

. . .

I meet Mike in Nashville. I walk into his office, we shake hands, and I take a seat across from him.

"I got to tell you a story," he says. He's grinning but for some reason, I don't think he's about to tell me a funny story.

"Yesterday, I called thirteen people in Nashville. I kept track. I

called the thirteen people I consider the country music tastemak-
ers, the people who run this town. The influencers. My friends. I
told them I was signing you to a record deal."

He pauses. The grin fades. Mike shakes his head.

"Twelve of the thirteen told me it will never work. Twelve out
of the thirteen."

I fidget. I don't know where Mike's going with this, but I feel
a knot in my stomach.

"Only one guy said, 'Yeah. I get it.'"

"Who?"

"Frank Rogers."

Frank Rogers. Legendary producer and songwriter who has
been producing Brad Paisley for close to a decade. They've had ten
number one country hits together.

"Just one said yes," Mike says.

"More than enough," I say.

The grin returns to Mike's face.

"Exactly. All you need. One. The right one. If it's okay with
you, I asked Frank to be your producer."

"That works," I say, and then Mike leans into me and says,
"Darius, I don't care what anybody says. You give me a record, I'll
give you a chance."

. . .

To be honest, I'm not sure I would give myself a chance. If I were
president of a record company and if my own brother had a career
equivalent to mine, and asked me, *Hey, bro, give me a record deal to
make a country album,* I would say no. Forget the racist part of it.
Based on the non-racist part of it, I'd say no. Here's this guy, the
lead singer of a pop band that was huge for a minute, but that's over.
He had his fifteen minutes. That's it. Done. People in the country
world won't cross over. They won't buy in. It's not going to work.

But we do have to face the second part. The racist part.

It's 2008. How many Black artists have had a country hit in the past twenty-five years, since Charley Pride?

None. Zero. Not one.

Accident? Coincidence? Bad luck? I don't think so. I'm certain the powers that be in country music have purposely kept Black artists out of the business after Charley Pride. The way it is. Sad, but true. Why would the country music world suddenly open their doors to me and put me on the radio? Why me? Why would I be The One? I am facing an insurmountable hill to climb. Beyond a hill. Mount Fucking Everest.

So, why even try? Why set myself up for heartbreak and failure?

I don't know.

I guess I'm a fool who believes—in Doc, in Mike, in the record label, in myself, and in my songs.

I keep saying, it's about the music.

Always.

Every time.

. . .

Frank and I hit it off right away. Without saying a word, we connect, as if we're on a mission, two guys against the world. A couple days in, I loosen up and go with the flow. Now we're just a couple of guys hanging out in a recording studio, writing songs, making music, laying down tracks. It feels natural. It's actually more than that. Every day is a trip. Completely joyful. I'm having such a blast, I want to pinch myself. I can't remember when I've had more fun in a recording studio. I know the odds I face, but I feel zero pressure.

"I'm just doing this for the music," I continually remind myself and Frank.

"Only reason to do it," Frank says. "For the music."

"Okay, if I'm honest, I want the album to be good enough that they'll let me do it again. That's it. No pressure."

"Modest goal," Frank says.

"That's all I want."

It really is, but luckily we also have help from some of the best studio musicians in Nashville, and a couple of all-stars pop in to play and sing. Brad Paisley joins in on "All I Want With Me," and Vince Gill and Alison Krauss sing with me on "If I Had Wings." Frank and I keep our heads down, keep working, laying down tracks, and after we finish "Don't Think I Don't Think About It," Frank says, "Darius, this record is going to be a hit."

"Right," I say. "Going to fly up the country charts."

"I'm telling you," Frank says.

Then we record a very personal and emotional song, "It Won't Be Like This for Long," inspired by watching my daughter Dani grow up way too fast. I remember Beth and me taking her to preschool when she was three. We stood outside the school, Dani between us, clinging to my leg. She didn't want to go inside. Finally, reluctantly, she agreed to give it a try. We went in with her and after a while, she allowed us to leave her with the other kids. After school, she ran over to us. I bent down and asked her, "How was school?" She burst out crying. "You guys left me all day with a bunch of people I don't know." By the end of the first week, she'd basically forgotten about us. She'd made friends and didn't want to leave school. What happened to that little girl a week ago? Yeah, I thought, it won't be like this for long.

After we lay down that track, Frank says, "Darius, I'm telling you, this record is going to be a hit. Dads and daughters will be dancing to this song at weddings."

And after we record "Alright," Frank says, "Darius, this song is going to be huge. It's a hit."

"Frank, you say that every day, after every song."

"I know I do," Frank says. "And I mean it."

. . .

Then, one day, we cut our last song. The recording sessions end. The smoke settles, literally, in the control room and I realize that I've actually done it. I have recorded my country album. Working with Frank has been a dream and recording the album is a dream come true. What's more, we've made a real *country* album. Can't explain how I know. It simply sounds and feels like a country record. It just does. I have tried to channel Radney Foster's voice the whole way through. His voice echoes in my head. To me, its the essence of country music—clean, strong, soulful—what I have been striving to sound like. I hope I've come close.

Meanwhile, we need to come up with a name for the album. We toss around ideas. Thoughts of both starting over and learning something new come to mind. Finally, one phrase sticks and we have our title. We call the album *Learn to Live*.

Capitol proposes to release the record in early fall, a month after we finish the final Hootie tour. The timing seems right although the reality of releasing the record at all still seems surreal to me. *Is this really happening?* I guess I'll believe it when I see my album in Sounds Familiar, or some other mom-and-pop record store. In the meantime, we talk singles. The label chooses "Don't Think I Don't Think About It" as the first single, which surprises me. I expect they'll go with something more upbeat, like "Alright." Instead they choose a ballad, always chancy because so many ballads come out at once that it's hard to get yours on the radio. It's like trying to squeeze inside a crowded field, hoping to find a spot on the airwaves. And not only is "Don't Think I Don't Think About It" a ballad, it's so completely *country*. I sound miles away from Hootie. I love that, but remember, not only am I a country singer now, I'm also still Black.

. . .

Mike wants me to hit the road.

"A radio tour," I say, digesting the idea.

"We want to set you up with all the big country stations in the South, Midwest, everywhere. You'll go out on the road and meet all the major DJs, program directors, media people, and introduce 'Don't Think' and a couple other songs to them personally. Mainly, we want to get these DJs to play the single."

"Hand sell it," I say.

"Exactly. The personal touch."

"Uh huh," I say.

Mike hesitates. "What do you think?"

"How long for the radio tour?"

Mike shrugs. "Couple, three weeks. Maybe four, five."

"Five weeks," I say.

"Six weeks tops."

"Six weeks on the road. How many radio stations are we talking about?"

Mike reaches for a paper on his desk and slides it toward me.

"A hundred stations," he says.

"A hundred and ten," I read on the paper he's sent over to me.

"I rounded down," Mike says. "I didn't want to scare you off."

I laugh, then I study the list in front of me. "Doing some quick math, if I go out five days a week, you're asking me to hit three radio stations a day. Give or take." I pause. "That's a lot."

"It'll be worth it," Mike says.

I hesitate for less than a second. "I'm in."

. . .

In my mind, two tours colliding.

The radio tour for my first country record.

The final tour for Hootie & The Blowfish.

Both seem unreal, almost as if they're happening to somebody else. One signifies an ending, overflowing with memory, nostalgia, joy, and sadness. The other signifies a beginning, punctuated by redefinition, a feeling of accomplishment, a touch of fantasy, and *hope*.

Also, a feeling of triumph.

I've done it.

I have my country album and I have my first country single.

I expect nothing.

I psych myself up—*Go out there. Hit the road. Go to those radio stations. Get them to play your record. They'll love it. They will absolutely love it.*

But expect *nothing*.

. . .

Mike Dungan never backs down; his support and encouragement never waver. But I continue to hear rumblings, echoes of doubts of "This can never work" from those twelve country music influencers who Mike contacted before he signed me to a record deal. I want to prove them all wrong, of course, but I don't blame them. I get it. I really am the new guy in town, arrived so recently from the land of pop music.

As we come to the end of the final tour with Hootie, I start talking about the single "Don't Think I Don't Think About It" in interviews. I don't sell the single hard, but I mention the upcoming radio tour. Then after our tour manager schedules a private event for the band in San Antonio, the label calls me. My contact for the radio tour says, "Hey, as long as you're going to be in San Antonio, fly in early and go to the big country music station there. I've set it up. Talk to George, the program director. They all want to hear the song and do an interview."

A week before the event, I drop in to the label's offices to get my itinerary. I take my seat in the conference room with several suits from Capitol, waiting for Mike to say hello.

I hear him before I see him.

A door bangs. A curse strafes the halls. Footsteps wham on the floor, coming louder, closer, and then Mike blows into the conference room like a human tornado. His face pulses a deep, shocking crimson. I'm seriously afraid he might explode. He snaps a sheet of paper he's holding in his hand.

"What. The. *Fuck*?" he screams.

Silence. Nobody speaks because everybody knows Mike is just getting warmed up. "*Why* the *FUCK* would *y'all*—"

He's so livid he can't complete the sentence. He stops, holds, then roars again, "I cannot believe y'all are sending him to *Texas*. You shitting me? You know how Texas is with country music. They're not going to play him until *everybody else is playing him*. Texas is not going to be the one to break this."

Then he drops his voice so low I have to strain to hear him, which makes what he says even more emphatic.

"You are sending him into a bad situation."

Then he revs himself up again and screams loud enough to shatter glass, "Why the fuck would you send him there *first*?"

Of course, the *him* he's talking about is sitting and squirming at the far end of the conference table.

Me.

The him is me.

. . .

Eventually, Mike decides that it will be even worse for us to cancel the San Antonio interview so he cools down. A week later, I leave for the radio station with Jimmy Harnen, the representative from the label, a guitarist who'll accompany me on acoustic guitar, and a feeling that this first tour stop can't possibly amount to much. It doesn't matter. I'm just pumped about going on the road: me, the newly minted country singer, traveling with my own guitar picker, a bunch of new songs I want to present to the world, and an album on the way.

. . .

At the radio station in San Antonio, Jimmy and I follow a station employee into a glass-walled conference room where four higher-ups await—Hootie fans, I know, because they tell me. A round of handshakes, well-wishes, and then a fifth person from the station joins us: George, the program director, in a pressed cowboy shirt and bolo tie, a guy I've met. We talk sports and music, surefire and safe conversation starters, and then by design, to give the full effect of the song—no live acoustic version this first time—Jimmy pops the CD into their stellar sound system and "Don't Think I Don't Think About It" rains over us through throbbing bass-heavy ceiling speakers, filling up the room. As I sit in the corner, waiting for a reaction from the room, I realize I'm holding my breath.

The reaction comes almost immediately, right after the first chorus.

Five people sharing one smile.

That's what I see, what I feel.

Everyone grinning, bobbing their heads, tapping their feet, all of them *smiling*.

They love the song.

The song finishes, and they applaud.

I want to scream, *HOLY FUCKING SHIT,* but I stumble through a murmured, "Thank you."

"That's a great song," someone says, overlapping with someone else's "What an awesome song."

"I *love* it," George says. "Darius, dude, I love this." Then he turns to the others in the room as if I'm not there, and says, "Guys, I love this, I love Darius, I love this."

Then he pyramids his fingertips below his bolo, pauses, and says, "I'm going to add that record today."

Today?

I do not expect this.

Texas is not going to be the one to break this.

"That's fantastic," Jimmy, the guy from the label, says, and then the higher-ups in the room trip over themselves, gushing over the song again, and then somewhere in the center of the lovefest in that room, Jimmy clears his throat and says, "But, hey, only thing, can we wait? We have a big ad week coming up in two weeks and a big ad day during that week. Can you wait until then? We would love that. That would be better. That would be ideal."

George nods and says, "Of course. We can wait."

We plan on staying at the station for an hour, but we spend the whole day, hanging out. At one point, back in the conference room, I play two or three more songs from the album and "Let Her Cry." NPR has just created "Tiny Desk Concerts," and that's exactly what it feels like I do that day, my own abbreviated acoustic mini concert, twenty minutes in a radio station, just me, my voice, and a guitar. And that day, not being able to help themselves, the station plays the song, an exclusive, a sneak preview, one time only, "the first time you'll hear Darius Rucker's new song anywhere, that's Darius Rucker, solo, and now here's *Darius* . . ."

Later that afternoon, as we get into the car, Jimmy's phone rings. It's George.

"Hey, man, turn on the station. I'm adding 'Don't Think' right now. I have to do it. The first time we played it, the reaction was nuts. Calls flooded in. We're playing it, man. People love the song."

That's when I know—despite all the doubts, rumblings, and racism.

I know I have a chance.

My country music career might actually work.

. . .

The Hootie tour ends. Our final tour. Our final show. That's pretty much all I can say because that's all I remember. I look back and I see a blank black wall. I know that we don't break up, officially or unofficially. We say nothing about that. We don't call it quits. We don't say goodbye. We leave every door open.

I can imagine, as we pack up our stuff for the last time, all of us prepared for this moment without being prepared at all, a series of clichés, the obligatory "See you soon," "Call you," "It's been great," even future plans discussed. I visualize hugs all around, the four of us, then hugging our road crew and everyone who makes us go, onstage and off. Who *made* us go. Past tense. Maybe some tears? I don't think so. Anger? Not that I remember. No emotional outpouring. We've been through too much, together and separately. And, yes, I admit—denial. That has to be the emotion I feel most. I can't admit it's over. I will see these guys, I know I will. Especially Dean. I'll see Dean. And, yes, Mark and Soni, *yes*. Not sure when, but I'll see them. I know I will.

I stretch into my memory, I squeeze into the past with all I've got, I try to remember—and I cannot dredge up that night. Can't do it. I refuse to accept an end, the end, our end.

I do remember leaving, not lingering backstage because I'm hitting the road first thing in the morning. We've launched the radio tour for "Don't Think I Don't Think About It" and tomorrow I'm heading to Boise, or Wichita, or Sioux Falls, or maybe all three. Impossible to keep track. I love playing the songs live, going one-on-one with DJs, playing "Don't Think" in tiny, cramped spaces across the control panel, my body practically pressed into the door, almost literally no room to breathe, then starting to sing and watching the DJ's face light up, the room crackling with sound, the strumming guitar, the echo of my voice. I hear my fair share of, "Man, Darius, I love that song, I love it, but my audience, you know, I just don't know if they'll accept—"

Stop. Stop right there. I get it. I mean, I don't get it, but I get what you mean. It fucking sucks, but I'm in—fill-in-the-blank/deep redneck country here—and I'll just pack up my guitar and my song and go. Don't want to force my music or anything else on anyone.

But—most people don't say that.

Most DJs let the song speak. They listen to the song, they *hear* the song, they love the song, and they add it, instantly.

Which is why on May 3, 2008, "Don't Think I Don't Think About It" debuts at number fifty-one on the Billboard Hot Country Songs chart. Out of nowhere.

The next week the song creeps up a few notches, and the following week it moves up again, not a meteoric rise, but a slow, steady climb, which, frankly, I prefer. I don't want to be a shooting star that blazes hot, bursts into flames, dissolves into dust and disappears. I want a slow, lasting heat, an indelible burn, my song leaving a mark.

That's what happens. I play the radio tour, going from town to town, radio station to radio station, a modern-day troubadour, singing for my song, for recognition, for entry into the country music club, "Don't Think" trying to scratch its way into the canon. Most stations welcome me, embrace me, and add the song. Then summer melts away, the label releases the album *Learn to Live* in mid-September, and a few months later the world, which has identified me as Darius Rucker, lead singer of Hootie & The Blowfish—the world changes, I change, and to my shock, I am reborn as Darius Rucker, country singer.

. . .

October 3, 2008.

My mind usually jumbles dates, but this date I know for sure. It's permanently etched into me, like a tattoo.

I sit in the close quarters of a radio station, WQYK in Tampa, Florida, two feet across the control panel from a DJ I know pretty well. He's had me on before for "Don't Think I Don't Think About It," but now the song has been scorching since the album release a couple weeks ago, reaching all the way to number two, falling back three slots, then reversing course and hitting number two again.

I have completely bought into the radio tour concept, although we've officially blown through those initial 110 tour stops. We tour now as needed and by choice. I love this station, this DJ, a Hootie fan and early supporter of my country career. On air, as I cradle my guitar, we talk about the song again, and as I absently tune my guitar to play it live, the DJ and I reminisce. He says, "Been a while since I've seen you. I remember when you introduced your song right here, in this studio. Blew us all away."

"Yeah, I remember that. My first country single. You never know how that will go."

"Very true. So, how do you feel about having a number one record?"

I blink. I'm not sure I've heard him right.

"What do you mean?"

"Tomorrow morning, when the new charts come out, 'Don't Think I Don't Think About It' will officially be the number one song in country music."

I stare, frozen in time, my face feeling like a cement mask, and then I lose it. My eyes fill with tears and I start to cry. Within seconds, I am blubbering like a baby, sobbing on the radio. Live.

I feel shock. I feel relief. I feel humbled.

I want to scream, *I did it! I've made it as a country singer!*

But I just keep crying.

At some point, through my tears, the massive importance of this moment hits me. I am the first solo Black artist to have a number one country music record since Charley Pride sang "Night Games" in 1983, twenty-five years ago.

Then I catch my breath and the doubts swim in again.

I'm dreaming. Or this is a fluke. Or a mistake. An aberration, a one-week-only, one-time-only, once-in-a-lifetime occurrence, like seeing a unicorn.

No. I'm wide awake. I'm here, alive, awake, in the flesh. I know because I actually pinch my forearm and it hurts.

And it's not a fluke. It's real. The DJ passes me a printout of the charts and I see for myself, in black-and-white and slightly smudged. "Don't Think I Don't Think About It" sits at number one, set apart and in larger, bolder font than the ninety-nine songs below it.

It's not a mistake. The Hot 100 chart tallies sales from record stores. It's accounting. It's calculation. It's math. The rankings are based on numbers and the numbers don't lie.

It's not an aberration, not a onetime thing.

The following week, "Don't Think" appears at number one again.

A few weeks later, we release "It Won't Be Like This for Long" and that hits number one for three straight weeks, and after that, we release "Alright," which lands at number one for another two weeks.

I'm humbled. Beyond humbled. I'd just wanted the country music world to listen to my music and give me a chance.

I've gotten that and more, more than I ever thought possible. I have three consecutive number one singles.

It doesn't stop there. *Learn to Live,* my first country album, debuts at number one on the Billboard Top Country Albums chart, and hits number five on the overall Billboard Top 200. The album—my first country album—will sell over one million copies and become certified platinum.

There's more.

In 2008, I perform at the Grand Ole Opry for the first time. I hit that stage and before I launch into "Don't Think I Don't Think About It," I shudder. At first, I think someone has turned the air-conditioning too high, but then I realize I have chills. I'm standing on that legendary stage, singing through goose bumps.

Then, I receive my most gratifying honor. The Country Music Association honors me with the 2009 Best New Artist Award. In the forty-three-year history of the CMA, I am the first African American to win the award.

And, yes, when I hear the news, I cry.

21

"NEED YOU NOW"

Lady A

I am a country singer.

In my heart, I've always known that. My unexpected, stunning success with *Learn to Live* and my three number one singles have validated me. But it's happened ridiculously fast. I always doubted that the country music world would welcome me, but they have, and within only a few *months*. Still, I wonder. Is the welcome temporary?

I ask Doc about it.

"The country music fans like me—the critics liked my record—but does the country music community respect me?"

Doc takes too long to answer.

"Got to keep working," he says. "Keep writing good songs, putting out good music, keep getting better."

"That's a no."

"That's a 'you're just getting started.'"

"Fuck me," I say. "What do I have to do?"

"Off the top of my head," Doc says, "a Grammy would be a game changer."

In 2010, we step it up. I prepare to record my second country album with Frank Rogers again producing. But before I go into the recording studio, Doc calls to tell me that I have been invited to sing at the Country Music Television awards show, televised live from Nashville. I'm all in. Then Doc hits me with news that knocks me back. The CMT producers want me to sing the biggest country hit of the year, "Need You Now," onstage, in front of Charles, Dave, and Hillary, better known as Lady A, who wrote and recorded the song. And they want me to sing it with twenty-two-year-old British singing sensation, Adele.

As I say, I love duets. I love blending my voice with other voices, and over time I share a mic with, among others, Willie Nelson and Bruce Springsteen, and sing duets with Lionel Richie, Keb' Mo', Radney Foster, the Black Crowes, Nanci Griffith, of course, and Reba McEntire, Katy Perry, and Sheryl Crow, who will become my Tammy Wynette.

But *Adele*?

She's twenty-two but she's on the verge of becoming one of the biggest stars in the world and—let's be honest—her voice is a freak of nature. Beyond angelic. Godlike. I listen to her sing—and I have many times—and the sheer size of her voice humbles me.

I know that performing at the CMT Awards represents scaling farther up that previously insurmountable country music mountain of acceptance. But the idea of singing with Adele, I have to admit, makes me a little nervous. So as I walk toward her backstage for rehearsal, I hear myself mutter, "Please don't let me suck."

I needn't have worried. Adele and I hit it off immediately. She's down-to-earth, funny, and genuine. We talk music, and while I won't label her a country singer, I tell her that I hear a combination of country and R&B in her songs. To me, her biggest hits, "Chasing Pavements" and "Cold Shoulder," are country songs. Turns out she loves country music. We rehearse "Need You Now" and I fight an urge to stand back and just listen to her sing.

. . .

The next night, the night of the show. Luke Bryan introduces us and Adele and I emerge from the wings, walk to our marks onstage, stepping under a shadowy blue archway that douses us in pale blue light. The band behind us goes into the "Need You Now" intro and Adele, fluttering her fingers, as she is known to do, starts singing, her voice soaring to the heavens—*"Picture perfect memories scattered all around the floor—"*

I don't know where I am.

I'm not even sure who I am.

I feel as if I'm in costume, dressed all in black—pressed black slacks, black sport coat over a black and gray pin-stripe shirt. For a second, I feel as if I have stepped out of my body—and then Adele's voice jolts me, brings me back to earth, and I sing with her, tentatively—

"It's a quarter after one, I'm all alone and I need you now . . . "

I picture Beth.

I see our kids.

I am all alone, in some hotel room, in some town, after a show, missing my kids, missing my wife, reaching for a bottle, and then my mind snaps back to reality—I'm gone for only a blink—and I look at Adele, standing and swaying three feet away from me, her eyes closed, and I belt, *"I wonder if I ever cross your mind—"*

Adele comes in. Our voices meld. The band plays and I let go, ad-libbing, singing, "Whoa, whoa, yeah, yeah," and Adele sings, her voice lifting us both, and I'm into this song now, into this moment, any hesitation falling away, and Adele and I belt together, *"Baby, I need you now,"* in perfect harmony, in synch, as one, and we soar together now, and we blow the fucking roof *off*.

We finish the song, we bow, I look beyond the floodlights into the audience and I see Lady A—Dave, Charles, and Hillary—on their feet, applauding, and then I see Hillary, her hands folded beneath her chin, as if in prayer, and I see that she is sobbing. She bows to us, to Adele, and to me.

Adele and me.

We own the stage.
We own the night.

. . .

October 12, 2010.

It has happened. I have gotten the chance to do it again.

Capitol releases my second country album, which I call *Charleston, SC 1966,* the year of my birth and a nod to my hometown, the place that holds my heart. I've been thinking about that title for years. I have vowed to honor Radney Foster and his album *Del Rio, TX 1959,* his title invoking *his* birthplace and birth year. Even better, a dream for me, Radney and I write a song together, "Might Get Lucky," that I include on the album. In the recording studio, I tell Radney again how much his music and his emotional singing style have meant to me. Only everything, I say. And on this album, I do get lucky. Two singles, "Come Back Song," which I write with Chris Stapleton and Casey Beathard, and "This," on which I collaborate with Frank Rogers and Kara DioGuardi, reach number one. The album itself hits number one on Billboard Hot Country Albums. Incredibly, I have now recorded two number one country albums and five number one songs. I keep trying to get my head around the transition I've made from pop to country and having actual *success.* Except for the small amount of, sadly, expected racist bullshit I receive—one of the typical if milder tweets reads, *leave country to the white folk*—I have been welcomed. Well, not completely. The country music club does have this thing about outsiders. But like Tammy Cochran sings, "I'm Getting There."

. . .

The years pass, 2010, then 2011. I tour, opening for Lady A, and Brad Paisley, and then I headline, drawing huge crowds, filling theaters and arenas of frenzied fans who spend the entire show on their feet, dancing and singing along to every one of my songs. Gripping the mic onstage, I say to myself, still somewhat in disbelief, *They know every one of my songs, every single word.* I keep asking myself—*This happened so fast, is it real?*

"Oh, it's real," Doc says. "You're a country singer. No. You're a country *star.*"

Then, at the end of 2011, I receive further validation.

I get a text from a friend I met at an awards show—a big star then, today the biggest musical attraction since The Beatles.

Taylor Swift.

About to turn twenty-two, Taylor has come to the last leg of her *Speak Now* world tour and asks if I'll sing "Alright" with her at her concert in Columbia, South Carolina. Practically my backyard. She'll bring me on as a surprise. All I have to do is walk down a staircase and meet her onstage. Easy. I'm all in.

All goes according to plan. Taylor's killing it, the crowd going insane after every song. As she's about to wrap up the show, she says, "You know my favorite country artist is from South Carolina, and I hope it's *'Alright'* if we have a guest tonight."

Wild applause as she whirls toward the staircase and I appear in a spotlight at the top.

Wilder applause.

We start singing the opening to "Alright." I take the first step, look down—toward the bottom of this long, ornate, gilded *treacherous* staircase—and one thought jumps into my head—

Please don't let me trip and fall down these fucking stairs.

But then Taylor's singing, and I'm singing, *"It's alright, and it's alright (alright) yeah . . ."*

I make my way—slowly, *slowly*—down the staircase, a step at a time, the crowd roaring, singing with us, the words to the song echoing, crashing down, cascading around us, and suddenly—whew—I'm on the stage, standing next to Taylor, swaying, singing, *"I got all I need,"* and I'm grinning, semi-delirious, the crowd out of their minds. We finish "Alright" and walk offstage, arms around each other, and I think, Damn, can't get much better than this.

. . .

And yet, it's still hard to feel that I'm a star, even as my songs are selling well, my albums are selling well, fans are coming out to my shows, and I'm sharing a stage with Taylor Swift. So, to keep it real, I keep going, hard as I can. With Doc guiding me, in 2012, we prepare to record my next country album. We've been invited to do this a third time, I marvel. For this album, as on the others, I collaborate on every song, writing many of them with Frank. We identify several that we think could be singles, including "True Believers," "Radio," and "Love Without You," a song I sing with Sheryl Crow. Then one day, I take a break from the recording studio in Nashville and head to Baltimore to watch my daughter Cary perform in her high school talent show.

Beth and I take our seats in the Jemicy School auditorium. We watch all the kids perform and of course Cary is fantastic. During intermission, as the student tech crew changes the set, the faculty band—two teachers, the principal, and the janitor—plays for us. The band starts playing a song I know well, but it takes a moment for me to recognize—"Wagon Wheel," written by Bob Dylan and Old Crow Medicine Show. I remember reading that Dylan wrote a thin sketch of the song nearly forty years ago for the film *Pat Garrett and Billy the Kid,* but the song never made it into the movie. Thirty years later, Ketch Secor of Old Crow Medicine Show heard a bootleg tape of the song, refined it, added new verses, and recorded a bluegrass version, which became a hit for them. Now, the Jemicy faculty band plays "Wagon Wheel" in an entirely different way—up-tempo, with twang, with heart, and with drums. I've never heard the song played like this. The faculty band has turned it into a straight-ahead country song. The song has never resonated with me. Until now.

"Holy shit," I say.

"What's wrong?" Beth says.

"This song," I say. I punch numbers into my phone and text Frank.

Wagon Wheel. Remember that song?

He texts right back. *Yeah. Why?*

I text him back. *I want to cut it.*

He texts me back. *Yeah. I don't know.*

I text him back.

I'm not asking. We gotta cut this song.

. . .

We cut it for the new album, but I add a secret ingredient, something special that elevates the song, raises the record to a higher plane. I get Lady A to sing background. Then in July, for the ninety-fifth anniversary of the Grand Ole Opry, I perform the song live with Old Crow Medicine Show themselves. We kill it, rocking the song, with Ketch patrolling the mic next to mine, harmonizing the chorus with me, stomping his feet like a man trying to put out a campfire, while absolutely violating his violin. During the musical bridge, lost in the music, I lose my mind. I step back, as each member of Old Crow Medicine Show takes a solo, and I shout, "Let's play some country music, boys!"

We finish the song, and as we take our bows, I become aware of the entire crowd roaring, rising to their feet, going insane. I swear I feel the stage shaking. I've experienced tumultuous reactions to live performances before, especially fronting Hootie. But I don't know if I've ever felt a crowd reaction like this. I absolutely *feel* it. From my feet to my gut to my head. Afterward, backstage, high from the performance and nothing else, I tweet a response about the Grand Ole Opry performance and my upcoming album—*Secret out after @opry perf. I recorded a version of Wagon Wheel for my new record and @ladya sings on the track.*

Not sure I'm supposed to break the story about my secret ingredient in a tweet, but I don't care. I've got this feeling about "Wagon Wheel" and I want the world to share it.

. . .

October 2, 2012.

Saturday night at the Grand Ole Opry. I'm onstage, performing, about to finish my set, which, of course, is being broadcast live. I'm going with "Wagon Wheel" as my closer, as surefire a finale as I've ever played. But before that, I've been told that the Opry has instituted a new question-and-answer feature. First I've heard of this and I listen to the Opry every week. Oh, well. I'm game. I answer two layup questions from people in the audience and then the announcer says, "We have time for one more. Yes. How about this man over here."

A tall guy wearing a large, stylish Stetson steps into the aisle and takes the hand mic. The crowd goes nuts and I start laughing. Everyone recognizes him immediately.

Brad Paisley.

"Oh, my goodness," I say, wondering where this is going, knowing for sure that I am about to get pranked. Live. But I love Brad and I go along, even as I break up.

"This is funny," I say, still laughing.

"I have two questions," Brad says. "First, are you still the worst poker player in the world?"

"Yes," I say. "I still lose money every time I play."

"Other question," Brad says. "Would you like to be the newest member of the Grand Ole Opry?"

"Oh," I say. That's all I can say. I have gone into momentary shock. For a moment I can't catch my breath. Then I find my voice. "No! You're kidding. Really? Tonight? *Yes!* Yes, I would. Whoa. WHOA!"

I back away from the mic, overcome with emotion, tears sliding down my cheeks. Then Brad bounds onto the stage and envelops me in a bear hug, squeezing the shit out of me, clutching me like the Jaws of Life. I gasp, unable to find words. I keep repeating, "Wow," over and over. Finally, Brad releases me and grabs the mic.

"Welcome him home, everyone," Brad says to the audience. "This is his new home right here."

I turn my back so the crowd can't see me crying. I exhale, desperately trying to compose myself. Then a rush of adrenaline kicks in, and I spin around, face forward, and step up to the mic. "I can't believe I have to play a song right now. I am so—so totally moved. Thank you."

The next thing I remember, I hear the applause for "Wagon Wheel." I don't remember singing the song, finishing the song, bowing, nothing. I just know that I'm suddenly backstage and there's Brad again, grinning, pumping my hand, hugging the hell out of me again.

"This is unbelievable," I say. "I had no idea."

"Well, everybody else knew. Doc. Frank. Beth—"

"Beth knew? I can't believe it. She never keeps a secret."

"Welcome in, brother," Brad says.

Two weeks later, on October 16, 2012, as I stand on the Grand Ole Opry stage, Vince Gill formally inducts me. I graciously, humbly, and emotionally accept. In my brief acceptance statement, I say, "Twenty years ago, I never would have believed I'd be standing here. This is such a special moment, a dream come true."

Pete Fisher, the general manager of the Opry, takes some heat for inducting me, only the second Black singer to be brought into the Opry. Most complaints don't mention race, at least not directly. The haters cloak it by saying that I'm too new to country music. Pete Fisher stands at a podium before the country music press and fires back.

"Darius's career speaks for itself," Pete says. "We base our induction to the Opry on career accomplishment. On the one hand, you can say we're coming to Darius very late in his music career—and we're coming to Darius very early in his country music career."

He pauses, allows that to sink in. Then Pete, a calm, Southern gentleman, says, pointedly, "This man has accomplished a tremendous amount. From his debut on the Opry stage just a few years ago, Darius made an impression on us that has lasted—and we believe it will last for many years to come."

I vow to play at the Grand Ole Opry as much as possible. I believe I have kept that promise.

. . .

We release "Wagon Wheel" as a single in early 2013. It takes a few weeks, but the song hits number one on Billboard Hot Country Songs and just keeps selling, week after week, selling so many copies it's like we're giving the record away. Over time, "Wagon Wheel" will become my biggest-selling single ever, outselling "Hold My Hand," "Only Wanna Be With You," and "Let Her Cry." The song helps propel my album *True Believers,* which comes out in May, to number one on Billboard Top Country Albums and number five on the Billboard 200. "Wagon Wheel" will be officially "certified diamond," one of only six country songs to reach *ten million* in sales, joining "Need You Now" in that elite circle.

It's official. I've made it. I am a country singer. I am a card-carrying member of the country music club. Being inducted into the Grand Ole Opry by Vince Gill after being invited by Brad Paisley proves that. What more can I ask for?

Not to be greedy, but I'd really like a Grammy nomination.

That would seal it.

I try not to obsess over this, or even speak about my desire for a Grammy aloud, although sometimes I let it slip and say, when I'm interviewed, that I believe with all my heart that "Wagon Wheel" deserves a nomination. In one interview, my passion gets the best of my common sense and composure and I blurt, "If 'Wagon Wheel' doesn't get nominated for a Grammy, country music is screwed."

A little strong, I admit, but it's how I feel. I won two Grammys with Hootie, twenty years ago, but getting a nomination now will further validate my place in the country music community. I know, I know. The odds are against me, even with the song's insane sales, not to mention the brutal competition I anticipate in the Best Country Solo Performance category, likely Miranda Lambert and Blake Shelton. But as Doc says, winning a Grammy would be a game changer, so I do think about it, talk about it, and maybe even obsess about it, a little.

As the day for the nominations arrives, I talk myself out of it. For all the reasons I've mentioned and for every reason you can imagine, I know I won't be nominated. Can't happen. Won't happen.

It happens.

I get nominated for Best Country Solo Performance for "Wagon Wheel."

I'm stunned. I truly am.

I check the other nominees in my category. Predictably, I'm up against Miranda and Blake, along with Lee Brice and Hunter Hayes. Tough competition. All great. Doubt I'll win. But it is nice just to be nominated. It *is*. And I will fly to Los Angeles and attend the ceremony, just in case I might, you know, win.

. . .

I never hear Cyndi Lauper read the winner in my category because I'm not in the audience. I'm on the fucking 405 or the 10 or some L.A. freeway, stuck in typical, horrific L.A. gridlock, turning the freeway into a five-lane parking lot. I'm not alone. Alicia Keys, the Imagine Dragons guys, and Pharrell Williams are all stuck in the same gridlock because they can't get to Staples Center either. They all arrive late. But my driver must be a Hollywood stunt driver because even with the freeway nightmare, he manages to get me to Staples Center within minutes of Cyndi Lauper announcing the winner of my category. I burst out of my car at the artists' entrance, slam through the doors, and streak down the aisle *after* Cyndi Lauper has read, "And the winner of Best Country Solo Performance—*Darius Rucker*!"

Applause rising, ebbing, cratering to an eerie silence.

"Well," Cyndi Lauper says onstage, looking at the contents of the envelope in her hand, realizing by the silence that I'm not there, now thrown off, fumbling through thoughts, deciding how to cover my absence, "I'm sure Darius thanks the academy, and all his friends and family, and his mom."

Exactly right, Cyndi.

I do thank the academy, and all those folks she mentioned, and more, including Radney and Nanci and Doc and Frank and Mike Dungan and Pete Fisher and the entire country music community, and everyone who contributed to our version of "Wagon Wheel," and, yes, I do, especially, thank my mom. I know she's looking down at me, beaming, her eyes tearing up, shaking her head, thinking, Son, I love you, but of all the times to be late.

"LIFE'S TOO SHORT"

Darius

A great novelist wrote that all beginnings are difficult. Endings, I find, are even harder.

. . .

January 25, 2014.

Los Angeles.

The Tonight Show with Jay Leno.

I stand onstage, preparing to sing my song "Miss You," a deeply emotional ballad. I've heard that Jay, a big country music fan, loves the song. But as I stand in the shadows at the mic, I feel a catch in my throat. Jay is saying goodbye. In less than two weeks, he will be walking away, not only from *The Tonight Show,* but from what millions see as his identity. I think of "Here Comes the Sun," the Beatles song from *Abbey Road,* written by George Harrison. Dean and I played that album constantly, hours at a time, and now, as I'm about to say goodbye to Jay, who has been a strong supporter of me and my country career, Harrison's lyrics flood into my mind—*It's been a long, cold, lonely winter . . . here comes the sun . . .*

Jay introduces me. I sing "Miss You" with all I've got. I can't see him at his desk, but later someone tells me that as I sang, Jay fought back tears.

Endings are a bitch, Jay.

. . .

Then another difficult goodbye.

Letterman.

April 30, 2015.

New York City.

The Ed Sullivan Theater on Broadway.

Three weeks before the final *Late Show with David Letterman*.

I can't believe Letterman is leaving. I have been watching him religiously for decades, since his morning show. I have gotten up to him and gone to sleep to him. Feels like I've spent my whole life with him. Now, he's ending his run. Calling it quits. This last month, Dave is treating every show like a final show, like he's taking a long, farewell tour, bringing back the guests who have meant the most to him, including Hootie & The Blowfish.

He has asked us to reunite and perform "Hold My Hand," twenty-one years after we first played the song on his show. Of course we'll sing the song again. We'd be honored, even though the four of us haven't spent very much time together in the past six years.

We've seen each other occasionally. We text, we talk, and we perform together every year or so, a few days here for charity, a festival there for fun. We try to hang out more, but we're wrapped up in our own lives, our families, and other time-consuming obligations. Soni and Mark have both gotten divorced and Soni has married Mark's ex-wife. I went to the wedding. Mark didn't. But that's Soni and Mark's story to tell.

Me? Well, it happened. I'm a country singer, all the way, playing gigs, playing golf, cutting country albums, and appearing at the Grand Ole Opry as often as I can. Last year, I released an album of Christmas songs, called *Home for The Holidays,* and I'm about to release my next country album, *Southern Style.* I'm moving as fast as I can. I have a lot more to do and much more to say. Want to get it all in. But time has a way of flying by. As it turns out, life is too short.

. . .

The four of us don't say much in the dressing room or as we take the stage during the commercial break. I approach the mic at center stage and glance at my bandmates, my brothers. We look older, but we've aged well. We've cleaned up, too, in every way. I have shaved my head, and so has Soni. Dean is wearing glasses and a dark button-down shirt. He kind of looks like the accountant he never became. Mark wears a button-down over a white T-shirt. I wear a blue denim button-down loose over a pair of freshly pressed jeans. I also shined my boots for the occasion. We first played this song, on this stage, when we were four scruffy, hungover, clueless kids. Look at us now. We're survivors. Literally. We made it out alive. And now we've morphed into four legitimate, card-carrying adults.

The lights come up on Letterman, sitting at his desk. He seems buoyant, bordering on giddy, almost as if he can't contain his excitement.

We've appeared on his show so many times, and this will be our last time, I think. This is it.

Our last *Letterman* show.

Feels momentous . . . and sad . . . and the end . . . of something. Of an era. Of a time in all of our lives.

I can't imagine how ending his show feels for him.

I look at Dean to my right, his hands on his bass; Mark at my left, fingers on the frets of his guitar; I glance at Soni behind me, settling behind his drum kit.

I think about what our last show might be.

What would that feel like?

I swallow. Slowly shake my head.

I don't want to know how that feels.

I don't ever want to know.

I will never know . . .

Letterman speaks, jolting me.

"Our next guests made their television debut—listen to this— back in 1994. Their television *debut*."

He and his bandleader, Paul Shaffer, exchange a few words, expressing their disbelief, and then Letterman continues, "They will reunite for the annual Homegrown charity concert on August seventh and eighth, in Charleston, South Carolina. Performing the song that started it all—HOOTIE AND THE BLOWFISH!"

And then—

I'm singing.

The guys jump in, and we play the *shit* out of "Hold My Hand." We are so tight, so fucking *tight*. We have never sounded better, we have never played better. I sing and I actually feel goose bumps running up and down my arms. I am so lost in the song I almost don't realize when we finish. Letterman leaps up from behind his desk and strides over to us the way he did twenty-one years ago. He blazes a smile at us.

"How about that?" he shouts. "Oh, my!"

He looks at us, shakes his head, and says, "Oh, *man*. You sounded great in 1994. You sound better now."

David Letterman, the man who launched us, the man who made our career, who immortalized our name by speaking it every night on his show for a year, grips my hand.

"Darius," he says.

Then Dave says the sentence that I should say to him, four words that spring from his heart, the same words I vow that I will say to everyone close to me, for my final goodbye, whenever that moment comes, at a time far away.

"Thank you so much."

. . .

Looking back now, I close my eyes and once again, as always—

I'm singing.

Living my dream.

My destiny.

Doing what I was born to do.

Singing.

It's all about the music.

The *music*.

Always.

It's 2017. I'm in Nashville, cutting my album *When Was the Last Time,* working on something I wrote with Jaren Johnston, Jon Nite, and Ross Copperman, a song I call "Life's Too Short." The song's not what you think. It's not a sad song, or a song about regret, or lost chances. It's a rousing song, a party song, a song about living, about loving life.

I bring my lips an inch from the mic as I record this song, these lyrics my coda, this song, one I will add to my personal musical moments, a song I will include in my essential list of twenty-three—

And then—in my mind's eye, I'm a kid again.

I'm six years old, in our living room in Charleston, my mom's salt shaker in my hand, my pretend mic, my mom and her friends clustered at the edge of the couch, leaning toward me—

Because I'm *singing*.

I blink and I'm back in the recording studio—

Singing.

Words rushing out, the lyrics to "Life's Too Short."

"Tunes pourin' outta that slidin' rear window

Laugh to the beat of that tape deck radio

Mmm, it's a heaven on earth moment"

I press my eyes shut and allow this final song to engulf me, to swallow me—

And I'm singing.
"Life's too short just to like it
So, you better get to lovin' this living before it's gone."
I'm *singing.*
Yeah.
Life *is* too short.
Way too short.

PHOTO CREDITS